HEBREW FOUNDATIONS OF THE CHRISTIAN FAITH

BY

DAVID HAMSHIRE

Hebrew Foundations of the Christian Faith by David Hamshire

Published and Printed in Great Britain in 2017.

FAITHBUILDERS PUBLISHING

www.apostolos-publishing.com/faithbuilders

An imprint of Apostolos Publishing Ltd, 3rd Floor, 207 Regent Street, London, W1B 3HH

www.apostolos-publishing.com

British Library Cataloguing-in-Publication Data: A catalogue record for this book is available from the British Library.

ISBN: 978-1-910942-74-1

Cover design by Blitz Media, Torfaen.

Cover Image © Howard Sandler | Dreamstime.com

To contact the author, please write to: Apostolos Publishing Ltd, 3rd Floor, 207, Regent Street, London, W1B 3HH:

Printed and bound in Great Britain by Marston Book Services Limited, Oxfordshire.

The stone which the builders rejected has become the chief corner stone.

This was the Lord's doing;
It is marvelous in our eyes.

(Psalm 118:22–23).

CONTENTS

FOREWORD..6

INTRODUCTION 8

STUDY 1 — THE EXODUS FROM THE GARDEN
OF EDEN AND FROM EGYPT...10

STUDY 2 — JOSEPH AND JESUS....................................38

STUDY 3 — THE ARK OF THE COVENANT.............62

STUDY 4 — THE TABERNACLE....................................90

INTRODUCTION TO STUDIES FIVE – NINE........ 118

STUDY 5 — WHEN WAS JESUS REALLY BORN?.. 120

STUDY 6 — PSALM 23 136

STUDY 7 — HANUKKAH 152

STUDY 8 — OUR HIGH PRIEST.................................. 164

STUDY 9 — CREATION WEEK................................... 179

WHAT'S IN A NAME? 210

ANSWERS.. 214 - 227

ABOUT THE AUTHOR.. 228

BIBLIOGRAPHY 232

ACKNOWLEDGEMENTS

First I would like to thank Yahweh – the Hebrew name for God – for helping me with these studies. Although these studies were prepared for the benefit of others, my own faith has been greatly strengthened by studying and seeking out biblical truth as contained in God's Word.

I thank Dr. Ron George (together with his wife Nancy, founders of the Eurasia Education Foundation) for inviting me to join him in Moldova to present these studies to students at the Universitatea Divitia Gratiae (translates as: *'The Riches of His Grace'*) in Chisinau (Khisinev), the capital of Moldova.

I thank Dr. Mihai Malancea, his teaching colleagues and their staff, for welcoming me to the faculty in Chisinau. The ten days I was with them and their students was a great privilege; one I shall never forget.

I thank Mark Aldridge for proof-reading the manuscript and Niall MacTaggart for writing the Foreword. Mark and Niall, friends of Dr. George – although I have not met either of them – have been a great help with their suggestions for the improvement of this book.

David Hamshire

FOREWORD

When I was invited to read the manuscript for this new book, I was impressed on a number of levels. David's book gives a thorough foundation upon which the new believer and student of the Bible can gain biblical orientation which points to Jesus Christ.

I have read similar studies of Old Testament themes which relate to New Testament theology, and so was particularly blessed that the focus was on Jesus Christ as the true revelation of the Old Testament. That there can be a temptation by authors to launch into a closed-circled theological explanation, without making and pointing to the real application – to the living out of the application in the power of the Holy Spirit – makes David's book highly relevant as a valuable resource.

It would appear in studying the topics contained in this book, one would want to make a culturally genuine and contemporary application in view of where one originates from; for students of the Bible might come from a diversity of backgrounds, such as the students in the university where David first presented these studies.

The presence of the Holy Spirit and the kingdom of God are themes which can transform the course of our study, and David's book will, with certainty, be helpful in equipping believers in living fully in God's economy.

The employment in this book of induction questions – to draw in the student to dialogue and thinking about the topics and the ramifications thereof – is important if we are to see God reveal His word to men and women, and not only pass on something of what we have learnt; though it may be perfectly valid.

The supremacy of the Spirit of Jesus is our portion if we come in humility and with open hands and hearts, not as our right or our due, but trusting in God's grace and knowing that God is a merciful and loving Father.

I believe the use of this book would be a wonderful complement to any syllabus of teaching and education in a seminary or Bible school setting. David's book gives form without bondage, freedom without license, and sends the right message of a biblical witness to the living Lord Jesus.

Niall MacTaggart
Spruce Grove, Alberta, Canada

INTRODUCTION

A major part of my life has been in observing how Jesus is portrayed in the Old and New Testament Scriptures. In the New Testament, Jesus is its focus, for without Him there would be no New Testament. For those who wrote the Old Testament Scriptures, they would have been looking ahead to when Jesus would make His appearance, and so their writings provide much of the background material for the New Testament.

To understand the New Testament, an understanding of the Old Testament is necessary, and so we should look upon these earlier writings as building blocks. The fact they are Hebrew building blocks is important, and is why Jesus so often referred to these ancient Scriptures.

At a Christian Resources Exhibition in Birmingham (2015), and in conversation with a stranger (albeit a Christian), we discussed at length the importance of the Hebrew building blocks of our faith. Following our discussion, Dr. Ron George – who lectures each year at a Christian university in Moldova – invited me to travel with him to Moldova to lecture to first-year students.

Dr. George's request was that I should prepare a series of studies to teach the students a few of the Hebrew foundations of the Christian faith. By referring to some of my earlier notes, plus adding to them, I thus prepared a series of nine studies for the students in Moldova.

Coming from a variety of backgrounds – some of the students were converts from Islam, others came from Christian families – what I found interesting was the number of countries the students represented. When I asked which country they were from, I was introduced to Kazakhstan, Kirgizstan, Moldova, Russia, Tajikistan, Ukraine and Uzbekistan. I suspect it is likely that most Westerners – myself included – would need to consult a map to know where some of these countries are located!

The studies featured in this book are the studies I prepared for these young people. Taken together, they are just an initial exploration into a few of the Hebrew foundations of the Christian faith.

Because the students expressed appreciation for these lectures (and the questions I prepared for them), I have decided to make them more widely available; hoping they will prove to be of benefit to others who may be interested in the Hebrew background of what Christians (and many Jewish people) believe.

David Hamshire
January 2017

STUDY 1 – THE EXODUS FROM THE GARDEN OF EDEN AND FROM EGYPT

From a biblical perspective, the two Hebrew festivals of Passover and Unleavened Bread celebrate the same event (Exodus 12:1–20). Passover recalls when God delivered the Children of Israel from slavery in Egypt. The Feast of Unleavened Bread – unleavened bread refers to bread baked without leaven or yeast – recalls a life freed from the effects of slavery to enable God's people to live a new way of life. In New Testament terms, without leaven means to be set free from sin (1 Corinthians 5:7–8). Therefore, and following their four hundred years of slavery in Egypt, the Children of Israel's life-changing departure conveys two lessons, both of which remain valid to the present day.

1. Passover – Deliverance from slavery.
2. Unleavened Bread – To live a new way of life.

For Jewish people, these first two times of remembrance not only recalls freedom, they also paved the way for them to renew their fellowship with God – who sent to them Moses. Again, in biblical terms, we can think of Moses as being the Children of Israel's deliverer, or saviour (a saviour sent by God); so very similar to the sending of Jesus to be our deliverer, our Saviour.

These two ancient Hebrew festivals also recall the start of the Israelites' journey to the Promised Land, a land God promised to give to Abraham and his descendants as an everlasting possession (Genesis 13:14–17).

Jesus and Two of His Disciples

On the day when Jesus rose from the dead, as He walked with two of His disciples on the road which led from Jerusalem to Emmaus, by referring to this same Moses (and the prophets), Jesus explained to them the events which had recently taken place in Jerusalem, when He had been crucified on the eve of Passover.

Luke wrote (24:32) that as He opened the Scriptures, their hearts burned within them. Metaphorically, they were so moved as to say: *"Our hearts were on fire!"*

Today we have access to these same Scriptures, and can ask the Holy Spirit to assist us in our understanding of Jesus. As we study the Old Testament, the Scriptures Jesus referred to, we see Jesus concealed. In the New Testament Scriptures, written after Jesus had ascended, we see Him revealed – but we need the two; both the Old Testament and the New Testament Scriptures.

For this study, I begin at the beginning (of time) and commence with the problem we have inherited, before considering the problem's solution – the Lord Jesus. I define the problem in this way: it is our separation from God and why this has become the norm for most people.

Next, I will go to the end and describe how the story ends. The reason for doing so is to see that God has not abandoned His original plan. For God to have done so, some might argue, could lead to an accusation that when God made us, His plan was doomed to failure because it was not long-lasting.

The reason I say this is because what God did in the beginning (God made man in His image that we might have fellowship with Him) may seem to some that His plan was not sustainable; it failed at the first hurdle when Adam and Eve sinned. So how has God revived His plan to restore the relationship He once had with men and women – both Jews and Gentiles?

How the Story Commences

Our story begins not with the first account of creation (Genesis 1:1–2:3), but with the second account (Genesis 2:4–3:24). Allow me to explain. In the first account, Adam and Eve are not named, and neither Eden nor the serpent are mentioned. The tree of life and the tree of the knowledge of good and evil are not mentioned, neither is the temptation or the fall of mankind referred to. And the need for personal atonement does not feature in the first account of creation but it does appear in the second account, when God killed an animal in order to provide Adam and Eve with a covering (a form of atonement) when they hid from God because they were ashamed of their nakedness (Genesis 3:7 & 21).

A careful study of the two accounts of creation suggests they may not be telling the same story, for it is not until the second account that the problem of mankind is introduced – disobedience – which is not described until Genesis chapter three.

What happened in Eden was that Eve was tempted and she disobeyed God. Eve then went to Adam and he also disobeyed God. They disobeyed by eating some of the fruit from the tree of knowledge of good and evil, something they had been told not to do.

How Eve sinned is revealing: She gave way to the same three temptations Jesus faced when He was tempted by the devil in the wilderness.

The Three Temptations Eve Faced (Genesis 3:6)

1. **The lust of the flesh.** Eve considered (with due diligence) how appetizing the fruit was for food.

2. **The lust of the eyes.** Eve saw the fruit of the tree was pleasing to her eyes.

3. **The pride of life.** The tree was also desirable; able to make Eve wise

As a result of these three temptations Eve, and then Adam, disobeyed God. But also, the three temptations Eve and Adam faced are the same three temptations we can be tempted with – which is why we need Jesus.

When God made man He made him: *'to do justly, to love mercy, and to walk humbly with your God'* (Micah 6:8). However, because: *'For all that is in the world – the lust of the flesh, the lust of the eyes, and the pride of life – is not of the Father but is of the world'* (1 John 2:16), separation from God became inevitable.

The Three Temptations Jesus Faced (Luke 4:1–13)

1. **The lust of the flesh.** To turn stones into bread.

2. **The lust of the eyes.** Jesus was shown all the kingdoms of the world and their glory. The devil then offered them to Jesus as a gift.

3. **The pride of life.** Jesus was challenged by the devil to show He was God's Son by throwing Himself down from the pinnacle of the temple; to become like Superman! Jesus, of course, knew – *'Pride goes before destruction and a haughty spirit before a fall'* (Proverbs 16:18).

But let's return to Eden, for when Adam and Eve were ordered to leave the garden, it was man's first *'Exodus'*. The reason they left was because of the tree of life, for had they eaten of its fruit they would have lived forever. This, of course, was something God could not allow, for having disobeyed God, they could not remain to become like God. *'Then the LORD God said, "Behold, the man has become like one of Us, to know good and evil. And* *now, lest he put out his hand and take also of the <u>tree of life</u>, and eat, and <u>live forever</u>" – therefore the Lord God sent him out of the garden of Eden to till the ground from which he was taken'* (Genesis 3:22–23).

How the Story Ends

Having looked at how our story began, let's consider (briefly) how our story ends, described in the final chapter of the Bible. *'"I am the Alpha and Omega, the Beginning and the End, the First and the Last." Blessed are those who do His commandments, that they may have the right to the <u>tree of life</u>, and may <u>enter</u> through the gates into the city'* (Revelation 22:13–14). For those who trust in Jesus, these words describe our entrance into God's presence (not so dissimilar to when the Children of Israel entered the Promised Land).

What we now need to do is consider how these book-ends are joined; what happened in the in-between time and how God has restored men and women to the right of fellowship with God they once knew. Eden was originally a *'Land of Promise'*, a land prepared by God.

The Exodus of the Children of Israel from Egypt

Because of Adam and Eve's disobedience, which led to a curse (Genesis 3:17), consider next the Exodus of Israel from Egypt, a land of a curse, and how Israel's Exodus looked ahead to a land of blessing, the Promised Land – a paradigm of the *'Land of Promise'*, Eden.

The Exodus of the Children of Israel from Egypt is a reminder of God's desire for us to overcome the effects of slavery (in today's terms it is our slavery to sin), for the Exodus and the Children of Israel's inheritance, the Promised Land, looked back to what happened in Eden thousands of years earlier; but then forward to the tree of life which will be featured once again at the end of the ages, when, *'there shall be no more curse, but the throne of God and of the Lamb shall be in it. And His servants shall serve Him'* (Revelation 22:2–3).

Abram and the Promised Land

'Now the Lord had said to Abram, "Get out of your country, from your family and from your father's house, to a land that I will show you. I will make you a great nation; I will bless you and make your name great; and you shall be a blessing, I will bless those who bless you, and I will curse him who curses you; and in you all the families of the earth shall be blessed." So they came to the land of Canaan [the Promised Land]. *Then the Lord appeared to Abram and said: "To your descendants I will give this land." And there he built an altar to the Lord, who had appeared to him'* (Genesis 12:1–7).

Later, before God called him Abraham (Genesis 17:5), God again spoke Abram. *'Now when the sun was going down a deep sleep fell upon Abram; and behold, horror and great darkness fell upon him. Then He said to Abram: "Know certainly that your descendants will be strangers in a land that is not theirs, and they will serve them, and they will afflict them four hundred years"'* (Genesis 15:12–13). Why did God inform Abraham, before he and Sarah had a son, that their descendants would serve a heathen nation for four hundred years?

Eventually Abraham and Sarah had a son and God told them to name him Isaac – meaning *'Laughter'*. Later, when Isaac was sixty years old, Isaac and his wife Rebekah had children and from the two (for they were twins), God told Rebekah that Esau the elder would serve Jacob the younger (Genesis 25:23).

Jacob's first wife Leah gave birth to six sons. (Rachel, Jacob's second wife, was at first unable to conceive). Jacob also married Bilhah and Zilpah, who gave birth to a further four sons. Eventually, God opened Rachel's womb (Genesis 30:22) and Rachel gave birth to two sons, the first of which she named him Joseph. The name Joseph means: *'JEHOVAH will add/increase'*.

Joseph's brothers hated him and so they sold Joseph to a group of Ishmaelites, distant cousins and descendants of Ishmael, who took Joseph to Egypt and sold him to serve in Potiphar's house. Eventually Jacob – God changed his name to Israel (Genesis 35:10) – his sons and their families, moved to Egypt because of famine. Israel means: *'Triumphant with God. One who prevails with God'*, but it would be a long time before the Children of Israel would experience this for themselves.

Initially Jacob (Israel) and his family were welcomed by the Egyptians (Gentiles), because Joseph was seen as a blessing (a saviour) by providing them with food. However, after Joseph and his brothers had died, a new Pharaoh came to power and when he saw the Israelites might pose a possible threat to the Egyptians; he set taskmasters over them and forced them to become their slaves. Thus began the four hundred years of slavery (a form of anti-Semitism) God had told Abraham about.

Some years later, as the Israelites continued to increase in numbers, Pharaoh ordered all the male infants to be killed (as Herod ordered the male infants in Bethlehem to be killed when Jesus was born). However, when an un-named couple had a son who they wanted to save, they placed him in an ark made of bulrushes (as Mary placed Jesus in a manger).

According to the Torah, the name Moses comes from the Hebrew verb: *'To Pull, or Draw Out'* (of water). Moses was given this name by Pharaoh's daughter who rescued him from the Nile (Exodus 2:10). Forty years later, when Moses tried to help one of his countrymen (a Hebrew), and killed his Egyptian oppressor (a Gentile), Moses was forced to leave Egypt.

Moses fled to Midian and married the daughter of the priest of Midian, Jethro. For the next forty years Moses lived in exile as a foreign refugee. One day, as Moses was looking after his father-in-law's sheep in the region of Mount Horeb, the mountain of God; the LORD spoke to Moses and told him to return to Egypt (Exodus 3).

God's call for Moses to return to Egypt was in response to the prayers of His people. For four hundred years the descendants of Abraham, Isaac, and Jacob had been forced by a heathen nation to work as slaves. Egypt had become for them *'A Curse'*. Moses later described what God did for the Children of Israel. *"But the LORD has taken you out of the <u>iron furnace</u>, out of Egypt, to be His people, an inheritance"* (Deuteronomy 4:20).

We now move to when Moses returned to Egypt to tell God's people to prepare to leave; but before they could do so, they were told they had to make a sacrifice.

The First Passover

'Now the Lord spoke to Moses and Aaron in the land of Egypt, saying, "This month shall be your beginning of months, it shall be the first month of the year to you. Speak to all the congregation of Israel, saying: 'On the tenth of this month every man shall take for himself a lamb, according to the house of his father, a lamb for a household. And if the household is too small for a lamb, let him and his neighbor next to his house take it according to the number of the persons; according to each man's need you shall make your count for the lamb. Your lamb shall be without blemish, a male of the first year. You may take it from the sheep or from the goats. Now you shall keep it until the fourteenth day of

the same month. Then the whole assembly of the congregation of Israel shall kill it at twilight. And they shall take some of the blood and put it on the two doorposts and on the lintel of the houses where they eat it"' (Exodus 12:1–7).

Why did God order Moses to tell the congregation of the Children of Israel that on the tenth day of the first month of their (lunar) year, they were to select a male lamb – or goat – and keep it for four days before killing it on the fourteenth day; and to then smear some of its blood on the doorposts and lintels of their houses? Why on the fourteenth day, before they left Egypt, did the Children of Israel mark their houses with the blood?

Later, at midnight (on the fifteenth day of the first month), the Lord *'Passed-Over'* Egypt, and where He saw the sign of the blood, no-one died. In the houses of the Egyptians, all the first-born sons died. The sign of blood was how God identified those who were His. In future years, Israel needed to be reminded of this blood token, that when the Lord passed-over them, their freedom from slavery had been God's enabling.

Since the time of the Exodus from Egypt, Jewish people have continued to look back to when the lambs were killed on the eve of their first Passover, and remember what God did for them. In Exodus 20:2 we read: *"I am the LORD your God, who brought you out of the land of Egypt, out of the house of bondage."*

The account of Israel's Exodus is well-known, including their miraculous crossing of the Red Sea, and what happened in the wilderness where the people spent forty years failing to go where God wanted them to go – to the land He had prepared for Abraham's descendants. Their future could have been so different if they had but trusted and obeyed God. However, we must move on to when the Children of Israel prepared to cross the Jordan to enter the Promised Land.

The Promised Land

'Then the Lord spoke to Joshua, saying, "Command the priests who bear the ark of the testimony to come up from the Jordan." Joshua therefore commanded the priests, saying, "Come up from the Jordan." And it came to pass, when the priests who bore the ark of the covenant of the Lord had come from the midst of the Jordan, and the soles of the priest's feet touched dry land, that the waters of the Jordan returned to their place and overflowed all its banks as before. Now the people came up from the Jordan on the <u>tenth day of the first month</u>, and they camped in Gilgal on the east border of Jericho' (Joshua 4:15–24). Note the day.

Once they had crossed the Jordan, Joshua ordered twelve men, representing the twelve tribes of Israel, to take large stones and set them up as a memorial for their children as the place where they had crossed the Jordan on dry land; to enter the Promised Land.

It is understandable why Joshua erected a memorial for the crossing of the Jordan on dry land – as their parents had crossed the Red Sea on dry land – but is it important <u>when</u> they crossed the Jordan? In Joshua 4:19, we are told they crossed the Jordon: *'On the tenth day of the first month'*. It was the same day they selected a lamb without blemish for Passover; what their parents had done forty years earlier, before they had left Egypt.

But now let us go back to the previous day, the 9th day of the first month. In Joshua 3:5 we read: *'And Joshua said to the people, "Sanctify yourselves, for tomorrow the Lord will do wonders among you."'*

To sanctify means: *'To consecrate, to be set apart, to be made holy'*, and this the Children of Israel did on the 9th day of the first month, the day prior to the Passover lamb being chosen. The following day, the tenth, they crossed the Jordan. Four days later, in the afternoon of the 14th day of the first month, *'Now the children of Israel camped in Gilgal and kept the Passover, on the fourteenth day of the month at twilight on the plains of Jericho'* (Joshua 5:10).

Jesus and His own Passover – John Chapter 12

'Then, six days before the Passover [this would have been the 9th day of the first month] *Jesus came to Bethany, where Lazarus was who had been dead, whom He had raised from the dead. There they made Him a supper; and Martha served, but Lazarus was one of*

those who sat at the table with Him. Then Mary took a pound of very costly oil of spikenard, anointed the feet of Jesus, and wiped His feet with her hair. And the house was filled with the fragrance of the oil. But one of His disciples, Judas Iscariot, Simon's son, who would betray Him, said, "Why was this fragrant oil not sold for three hundred denarii and given to the poor?" This he said, not that he cared for the poor, but because he was a thief, and had the money box; and he used to take what was paid in it. But Jesus said, "Let her alone, she has kept this for the day of My burial. For the poor you have with you always, but Me you do not have always"' (John 12:1–8).

Six days before Passover was when Mary took a pound of costly oil of spikenard and anointed the feet of Jesus. Mary then wiped His feet with her hair. Mary's act of reverence (and sacrifice) coincided precisely with what the Children of Israel were told to do, and on the same day, prior to them crossing the Jordon to enter the Promised Land. What Mary did and her timing – *and on the same day* – must have been inspired by God.

What Mary did for Jesus in anointing Him with oil and wiping His feet with her hair, was the same as what took place on the day before Israel crossed the Jordan to enter the Promised Land; the day before the Passover lamb was chosen. Who would have thought, centuries later, that Mary would have repeated this same act of sanctification – the setting aside of the Lord Jesus for

His death at Passover – that God had told Israel to observe in the days of Joshua, and on the same day?

When the Children of Israel crossed the river Jordan to enter the Promised Land, although they may have looked back on their four hundred years of slavery, and their forty years of wandering in the wilderness, and that those years had finally come to an end, they would not have known centuries later the days and times appointed for these events (by God), would feature in the lives of Mary and her Messiah, the Lord Jesus.

But why did these things happen, and in the same order? It was because they are basic to a Hebraic understanding of how Jesus can set men and women free from their sin, to lead a new life of trust and obedience.

Who Today is a Slave?

One of the things Jesus taught is that men and women are prone to sin; and sin has the habit of permeating all we do – as seen in what happens when you add leaven or yeast to bread flour. In Galatians 5:9, we read: *'A little leaven leavens the whole lump.'* In the Bible, sin and leavened bread are seen as being synonymous. Jesus said: *"Most assuredly, I say to you, whoever commits sin is a slave of sin"* (John 8:34). Because Jesus was and is righteous (Unleavened Bread), He became our Passover Lamb, to set those who are unrighteous free from their sin.

Paul in his first letter to the believers in Corinth, using the metaphors of Passover, leavened and unleavened bread, explains this parallel of life's true experience.

Paul wrote: *'Do you not know that a little leaven leavens the whole lump? Therefore, purge out the old leaven, that you may be a new lump, since you truly are unleavened. For indeed Christ our Passover, was sacrificed for us. Therefore let us keep the feast, not with the old leaven, nor with the leaven of <u>malice</u> and <u>wickedness</u>, but with the unleavened bread of <u>sincerity</u> and <u>truth</u>'* (1 Corinthians 5:6–8).

A Lamb for a Family, a Nation, the World

When Moses told each family (of Israel) to choose a lamb, the lamb became: *'A Passover lamb for a family'*, for it enabled the Children of Israel to be set-free from slavery – slavery had been for them a curse. The Exodus of the Children of Israel began when they crossed the Red Sea; but this was only the start of their journey.

In the days of Joshua when the lamb was chosen – and on the same day – the lamb became: *'A Passover lamb for a nation'* as the Children of Israel crossed the river Jordan to enter the Promised Land. But this was only the next stage of their journey, there was still much to do and obedience would be the key to their future of remaining in the Promised Land.

Following the anointing of Jesus by Mary (on the 9th day of the first month) as an act of setting Him aside for

His death (which took place five days later on the 14th) the next day, the 10th, Jesus walked into Jerusalem. As He did so, the people cried out and said: *"Hosanna! Blessed is the One who comes in the name of the LORD! The King of Israel!"* (John 12:12). What a timely entry this was, the day the Passover lamb was to be chosen; the day Israel had crossed the Jordan. Just before Jesus entered Jerusalem, Caiaphas (the high priest) said: *"It is expedient for us that one man should die for the people, and not that the whole nation should perish"* (John 11:50). What Caiaphas did not realise was that Jesus was about to become: *'A Passover Lamb for the world'.* When Jesus entered Jerusalem on the tenth day of the first month, it was because God had destined Him to become a Passover sacrifice; to set us free from our sin.

The Cross of Jesus (a *'Tree of death'* as opposed to the *'Tree of Life'*), looked to the future, and to the world, and has enabled both Jew and Gentile to be set free from their bondage to sin and to walk in newness of life.

Paul the apostle writes about this in Romans chapter six. What is astonishing is the number of times Paul refers to the bondage of sin and of us being set free from our sin. This chapter (perhaps more so than other passages), emphasizes the need to understand what Jesus taught. *"Therefore if the Son makes you free, you shall be free indeed"* (John 8:36). The freedom Jesus spoke of is the freedom of being set free from the curse of sin, as Israel was set free from the curse (or bondage) of Egypt.

Paul wrote: *'What shall we say then? Shall we continue in sin that grace may abound? Certainly not! How shall we who died to sin live any longer in it? Or do you not know that as many of us as were baptized into Christ Jesus were baptized into His death? Therefore we were buried with Him through baptism into death, that just as Christ was raised from the dead by the glory of the Father, even so we also should walk in newness of life. For if we have been united together in the likeness of His death, certainly we also shall be in the likeness of His resurrection, knowing this, that our old man was crucified with Him, that the body of sin might be done away with, that we should no longer be <u>slaves</u> of sin.'*

'What then? Shall we sin because we are not under law but under grace? Certainly not! Do you not know that to whom you present yourselves <u>slaves</u> to obey, you are that one's <u>slaves</u> whom you obey, whether of sin leading to death, or of obedience leading to righteousness? But God be thanked that though you were <u>slaves</u> of sin, yet you obeyed from the heart that form of doctrine to which you were delivered. And having been set free from sin, you became <u>slaves</u> of righteousness. I speak in human terms because of the weakness of your flesh. For just as you presented your members as <u>slaves</u> of uncleanness, and of lawlessness leading to more lawlessness, so now present your members as <u>slaves</u> of righteousness for holiness. For when you were <u>slaves</u> of sin, you were free in regard to righteousness.'

'What fruit did you have then in the things of which you are now ashamed? For the end of those things is death. But now having been set free from sin, and having become <u>slaves</u> of God, you have your fruit to holiness, and the end, everlasting life. For the wages of sin is death, but the gift of God is eternal life in Christ Jesus our Lord.' (Underlining to show pros and cons of being slaves).

The eternal life Paul speaks of in this passage – as Jesus also described for Nicodemus, *"For God so loved the world that He gave His only Son, that whoever believes in Him should not perish but have everlasting life"* – is what Adam and Eve would have continued with had they been able to eat of the tree of life in the Garden of Eden.

Disobedience, we know, brought sin into the world. We also know how the problem of sin has been resolved, through the death of Jesus, for He gave Himself as a righteous sacrifice at the time of Passover, thus enabling men and women to be forgiven their sin.

What has been a serious loss for Israel, when Israel had the opportunity to see these truths for themselves and to teach them to their children and their children's children; that after the death of Jesus, Stephen, who had been accused of blasphemy, reminded his accusers that their ancestors had served the Egyptians for four hundred years before God rescued them and brought them into the Promised Land. But did they listen? Unfortunately not, and Stephen was stoned to death.

However, there is a silver lining, both for Jewish people and for Gentiles. The apostle Paul wrote in his letter to the believers in Rome: *'For I do not desire, brethren, that you should be ignorant of this mystery, lest you should be wise in your own opinion, that blindness in part has happened to Israel until the fullness of the Gentiles has come in. And so all Israel will be saved, as it is written: "The Deliver will come out of Zion, and He will turn away ungodliness from Jacob; for this is My covenant with them, when I take away their sins"'* (Romans 11:25–27).

God's promise is to both Jews and Gentiles, but with a proviso: *'Blessed are those who do His commandments, that they may have the right to the tree of life, and may enter through the gates into the city'* (Revelation 22:14).

The Importance of the Exodus

From what we have observed in this study, what are the lessons we can acquire from these initial foundations of the Christian faith? We know the problem of sin can be traced to Eden, where because of disobedience, Adam and Eve had to leave the garden – *'A Land of Promise'* – and be banished to a land that was cursed (Genesis 3:17). For Adam and Eve, it was a shameful Exodus. Later, the Exodus of the Children of Israel from Egypt (Moses, as we have seen, described their experience in Egypt as an *'Iron Furnace'*), was entirely different, it was that they might go to *'The Promised Land'* – a land of blessing – but with God's reminder for obedience.

Is it a coincidence, or highly significant, that in the book of Malachi, in the last chapter and the last verse (and note the last word), we read: *'And he* [John the Baptist] *will turn the hearts of the fathers to the children, and the hearts of the children to their fathers, lest I come and strike the earth with a curse.'* John the Baptist was the prophet chosen by God to prepare the way of the Lord Jesus, the one who is able to set people free from the curse (the consequences) of disobedience.

This recalling of the earth being struck with a *'Curse'*, recalls what happened when Adam and Eve sinned and had to leave God's land and His presence.

The apostle Peter wrote concerning our attitude to life, and that we should always remember: *'Therefore gird up the loins of your mind, be sober, and rest your hope fully upon the grace that is to be brought to you at the revelation of Jesus Christ; as obedient children, not conforming yourselves to the former lusts, as in your ignorance; but as he who called you is holy, you also be holy in all your conduct, because it is written, "Be holy, for I am holy"'* (1 Peter 1:13–16). Peter was quoting from Leviticus 11:45. *"For I am the LORD who brings you up out of the land of Egypt, to be your God. You shall therefore be holy, for I am holy."*

Peter continued: *'And if you call on the Father, who without partiality judges according to each one's work, conduct yourselves throughout the time of your stay here in fear; knowing that you were not redeemed with corruptible things, like silver or gold, from your aimless conduct received by tradition from your fathers, but with the precious blood of Christ as a lamb without blemish and without spot* [Jesus, the Passover lamb]. *He indeed was foreordained before the foundation of the world, but was manifest in these last times for you* [and ourselves] *who through Him believe in God, who raised Him from the dead and gave Him glory, so that your faith and hope are in God'* (1 Peter 1:17–21).

This passage recalls (in part) the Exodus of the Children of Israel from Egypt. Peter wrote concerning the need for obedience, not wanting to go back to former things (such as Egypt), to become holy, which is why God brought Israel out from a pagan land. Furthermore, Israel was saved by blood, the Passover lamb, a lamb without blemish or spot. This is identical to how Jesus has saved His people from their sin – by His own blood.

Conclusion

What stands out in this study is what Mary did for Jesus. Her action was not in any way frivolous, and the same is true today. What we are motivated to do, or what we do because we love Jesus, is never wasted.

The next time you feel a need to visit someone, or help someone, try doing it! You may be elated when you go out of your way to help others. And if it concerns a stranger, try introducing yourself. It's a good way to begin and it will assure the recipient of your sincerity.

We have observed in this study how Mary was vilified by Judas Iscariot. Jesus, however, commended Mary for her devotion and her obedience (Joshua 3:5). Although I am sure Mary was not looking for praise for what she did, nevertheless, her love for Israel's Messiah (and the Jew and Gentile's final Passover Lamb), continues to be remembered two thousand years later.

'I am David'

One of my favorite quotations is from the film, *'I am David'*, based on the best-selling novel by Anne Holm. At a particularly difficult time for David, when he was incarcerated in a slave-labor camp in Bulgaria, a fellow prisoner says to David: *"If you are alive you can change things. If you are dead you can't!"* It is a simple truth, yet poignant enough for us all – including myself!

Confession Time

I remember a time when I did not cross the road to assist a man in need of help. Later I was ashamed, I may have been able to change things, but I didn't – and then it was too late. What if my attitude had been different; what good might I have achieved, not because I am good, but because God wants me to change things?

For Mary, there may have been a temptation for her not to act as she did, to hold-back. I'm sure there were some who felt embarrassed by what Mary did, for example Judas. But she did what she did, and I'm pleased for her.

When I received an email confirming I was to go to Moldova to present these studies to the students at the university, I felt fear; fear I was not up to doing what I had been asked to do. A few minutes later Janet, my wife, called me down for lunch. When Janet removed her yoghurt pot lid, she saw that printed on the inside of the lid was a quotation (another quotation!). Janet passed me the lid and said: *"David, I think this is for you?"*

Taking the lid from my wife's outstretched hand, I read: *'YOU ONLY REGRET THE CHANCES YOU DIDN'T TAKE!'* It's true, if we do nothing, if we hide the gift God has given us, if we disobey God, we will never know what God intended us to do.

By the way, I kept the lid!

****

On the next four pages there are fifteen questions which are based on this study. The suggested answers can be found on pages 214–215.

Study 1 Questions – The Exodus from the Garden of Eden and from Egypt

1. What does the Jewish time of Passover recall?

ANSWER: _____

2. On the occasion of the first Passover, Moses told the Children of Israel to bake unleavened bread. In New Testament terminology, what do unleavened bread and leavened bread represent?

ANSWER: _____

_____

3. Explain how Jesus relates to unleavened bread (bread baked without yeast being added).

ANSWER: _____

4. List five things that are mentioned in the second account of creation (Genesis 2:4–3:24), which do not appear in the first account of creation. (Genesis 1:1–2:3).

ANSWER: _____

_____

_____

5. What did God do in order to cover Adam and Eve's nakedness – their shame?

ANSWER: _____

6. What is the Bible's definition of covering a person's sin? Only one word is required. If you are not sure, please refer to Leviticus 16:34.

ANSWER: _____

7. According to Revelation 22:12–14, what must we do to gain access to the tree of life – access that was denied to Adam and Eve?

ANSWER: _____

8. When God told Abraham to go to a new land, He told Abraham his descendants would serve another nation. Which nation was this and for how many years did Abraham's descendants serve this nation? (Acts 7:2–7).

ANSWER: _____

9. Why did the Egyptians kill the male children who were born to the Children of Israel? (Exodus 1:1–22).

ANSWER: _____

10. On which day of which month did the Children of Israel kill the Passover lamb and then mark their houses by applying some its blood to the doorposts and the lintels? (Exodus 12:1–7).

ANSWER: _____

11. Complete the following sentence: *"I am the Lord your God, who…"* (Exodus 20:2).

ANSWER: _____

_____

_____

12. On which day of the first month did the Children of Israel cross the Jordan to enter the Promised Land? (Joshua 4:19). What else took place on this day? (Exodus 12:3).

ANSWER: _____

_____

13. What did Joshua tell the Children of Israel to do on the previous day? (Joshua 3:5). What day of the first month would this have been?

ANSWER: _____

_____

_____

14. In John's Gospel we read that Jesus entered the town of Bethany six days before the Passover celebration was observed (John 12:1). The date would have been the 9th day of the first month of the Hebrew calendar. Describe what Mary did for Jesus (verse 3), and how this was similar to what the Children of Israel did in the days of Joshua (and on the same day).

ANSWER: _____

_____

_____

15. In Romans chapter six, Paul describes for us what happens when a person is freed from their sin – as the Children of Israel were freed from being slaves to the Egyptians. In your own words, describe how Jesus has enabled you to walk in newness of life (Romans 6:4).

ANSWER: _____

_____

_____

****

STUDY 2 – JOSEPH AND JESUS

The interval between the closing of the Old Testament period and the commencement of the New is accepted as having been about four hundred years, and mirrors the four hundred years the Children of Israel were enslaved by the Egyptians. Their four hundred years of slavery in Egypt is still remembered by Jewish people as a time of a curse. The second four hundred year period might be described as a time of silence, for there was little in the way of a prophetic voice.

When Zechariah was performing his daily duties in the temple and his friends and family were waiting outside wondering why he was taking so long, but unknown to them he was chatting to Gabriel, who would normally have been standing in God's presence (Luke 1:19), I suspect their hypothesis was that prophets belonged to earlier generations, not theirs. About nine months later, when his son John the Baptist was born, the feeling in Jerusalem may well have been that God no longer had a word for Israel (and so prophets no longer had a role in Israel); therefore, if a new prophet appeared on the scene, suspicion as to his credentials would have been quite in order. About thirty years later, when two supposed prophets appeared (and within a few months of each other), the thoughts of many may well have been: *"Who is this John the Baptist and this Jesus? Are they prophets; for this is what some are suggesting?"*

For Jesus' disciples, as they began to preach the gospel of the kingdom of God, the only Scriptures available to them were the writings of the Old Testament, but this was in no way a hindrance, for many of the writers of the Old Testament period wrote about Jesus. This is why Jesus was able to say to His disciples: *"These are the words which I spoke to you while I was still with you, that all things must be fulfilled which were written in the Law of Moses and the Prophets and the Psalms concerning Me"* (Luke 24:44).

Knowing that Jesus is referred to in many of the Old Testament Scriptures, in this study I will explore how Jesus is pre-figured in the second half of the book of Genesis. I refer to Old and New Testament Scriptures as this is the way the majority of Christians have been brought up to consider the two sections of their Bibles; but in reality it is one book.

Most Jewish people do not accept the New Testament as inspired Scripture. Conversely, many Christians have a preference for the New Testament, rather than the Old Testament. Most Christians, however, will be familiar with passages such as Isaiah chapter 53 and Psalm 22 as being prophetic; that is they refer to Jesus. But there are many other passages in the Old Testament that feature prophecies concerning Jesus, especially in Genesis.

To turn to Genesis, the first book in the Bible, is to turn to the beginning, and is why in this study I would like for us to consider the person and life of Joseph, an archetype of Jesus.

Joseph – an Archetype of Jesus

One of the earliest portrayals of Jesus can be seen in the boy-slave turned ruler, Joseph. During His last few hours with His disciples, Jesus said He was among them as *'A Servant'*. A servant is what Joseph became after he was sold by his brothers and taken to Egypt, where he served in Potiphar's house. Later, when Joseph was falsely accused of attempted rape by Potiphar's wife, Joseph was imprisoned, where he continued to serve others. It was not until Joseph was released from prison that He became a ruler, second only to Pharaoh – but his life was still one of serving Pharaoh and the Egyptians; to save them from famine. But not only the Egyptians, Joseph became instrumental in saving his own people, the descendants of Abraham, Isaac, and his father Jacob, which included his brothers and their families.

In the Gospels, Jesus is shown as having four ministries. In his introduction to his commentary on Matthew's gospel, Charles Price gives a description of these four ministries. In Matthew's Gospel, Jesus is described as *'A King'* in Mark's Gospel, *'A Servant';* in Luke's Gospel He is portrayed as *'The Son of Man';* and in John's Gospel Jesus is shown as *'The Son of God'.*

Returning to Mark's Gospel, Jesus said: *"For even the Son of Man did not come to be served, but to serve, and*

to give His life as a ransom for many" (Mark 10:45).
Jesus described Himself as a servant (as Joseph served
in Potiphar's house, in a prison, and Pharaoh), but one
day Jesus will reign as *'King of Kings and Lord of
Lords'* (Revelation 19:16). Like Joseph who served
Pharaoh, Jesus reflected His Father's will.

In Genesis, from chapters thirty to fifty, we have a very
detailed biography of Joseph's life, ranging from when
he was conceived, to when he died. There is probably
more information about Joseph in Genesis than of any
other individual. The fact so much of Genesis is given
over to remembering Joseph, suggests he was not just
merely the great grandson of Abraham; but that an
additional importance is associated with Joseph.

I'm not suggesting Joseph had divine attributes, other
than having been called to a life of serving others.
Joseph had weaknesses, but the Bible shows that many
of the things which happened to Joseph, also happened
to Jesus. Was this so that when Jesus came, the Jews
might be helped in understanding He was their Messiah,
the Christ, as Joseph had been a saviour in Egypt?

For this study I have selected a number of parallels from
the lives of Joseph and Jesus. I have already referred to
two of them – the servant and princely natures of Joseph
and Jesus. There are many others, but for nearly all of
them, Jesus never set out to repeat any of Joseph's
experiences or his attributes in order to imitate Joseph,

and so pretend He was Israel's Messiah. It was how others became involved in the life of Jesus, and how they observed Him, which gave rise to the similarities.

In this correlation of the lives of Joseph and Jesus, I refer to Scripture to show how their lives compare. To observe other similarities which may assist us in our understanding of Jesus, I recommend a careful reading of the account of Joseph's life as found in Genesis.

To learn about Jesus by studying the life of Joseph may appear fanciful, but God often uses similar methods and we see examples of this throughout Scripture.

The sign of Jonah being in the belly of the whale for three days and three nights before being cast onto dry ground, and Jesus being buried in the ground for three days and three nights before He rose from the dead, is a classic example of how the lives and experiences of other biblical characters help us to understand Jesus.

1. **The conception and birth of Joseph and Jesus was miraculous.**

Joseph *'Then God remembered Rachel and God listened to her and opened her womb. And she conceived and bore a son, and said: "God has taken away my reproach." So she called his name Joseph'* (Genesis 30:22–24).

Jesus *'Behold, an angel of the Lord appeared to Joseph* [the foster father of Jesus] *in a dream, saying: "Joseph, son of David, do not be afraid to take to you Mary your wife, for that which is conceived in her is of the Holy Spirit. And she will bring forth a Son, and you shall call His name Jesus"'* (Matthew 1:20–21).

2. **The plots to kill Joseph and Jesus.**

Joseph *'Now when they* [his brothers] <u>saw</u> *him afar off, even before he came near them, they conspired against him to kill him'* (Genesis 37:18).

Jesus *'Then Herod, when he <u>saw</u> that he was deceived by the wise men ... sent forth and put to death all the male children who were in Bethlehem and in all its districts, from two years old and under, according to the time he had determined from the wise men'* (Matthew 2:16).

'And one of them, Caiaphas, being high priest that year, said to them, "You know nothing at all, nor do you consider that it is expedient for us that one man should die for the people, and not that the whole nation should perish"' (John 11:49–50).

3. **They were stripped of their clothing.**

Joseph *'So it came to pass, when Joseph had come to his brothers, that they stripped Joseph of his tunic'* (Genesis 37:23).

Jesus *'The soldiers, when they had crucified Jesus, took*

His garments and made four parts, to each soldier a part. Now the tunic was without seam, woven from the top in one piece. They said therefore among themselves, "Let us not tear it, but cast lots for it, whose it might be," that the Scripture might be fulfilled which says: "They divided My garments among them, and for my clothing they cast lots"' (John 19:23–24).

4. **They were sold for monetary gain.**

Joseph *'Then Midianite traders passed by; so the brothers pulled Joseph up and lifted him out of the pit, and sold him to the Ishmaelites* [distant cousins] *for twenty shekels of silver'* (Genesis 37:28).

Jesus *'Then one of the twelve, called Judas Iscariot, went to the chief priests and said, "What are you willing to give me if I deliver Him to you?" And they counted out to him thirty pieces of silver'* (Matthew 26:14–15).

5. **When Reuben went to look for Joseph, the pit where he had been placed was empty. When the women who had come with Jesus from Galilee went to the tomb where He had been placed, the tomb was empty.**

Joseph *'Then Reuben returned to the pit, and indeed Joseph was not in the pit; and he tore his clothes. And he returned to his brothers and said, "The lad is no more; and I, where shall I go?"'* (Genesis 37:29–30).

Jesus *'Now on the first day of the week ... they, and certain other women with them, came to the tomb bringing the spices which they had prepared. But they found the stone rolled away from the tomb. Then they went in and did not find the body of the Lord Jesus'* (Luke 24:1–3).

6. Joseph and Jesus were taken to Egypt.

Joseph *'They took Joseph to Egypt'* (Genesis 37:28).

Jesus *'Now when they* [the wise men] *had departed, behold an angel of the Lord appeared to Joseph in a dream saying, "Arise, take the young Child and His mother, flee to Egypt, and stay there until I bring you word; for Herod will seek the young Child to destroy Him"'* (Matthew 2:13).

7. A wild animal(s) was seen as having attacked Joseph and Jesus.

Joseph *'Then they sent the tunic of many colors, and they brought it to their father and said, "We have found this. Do you know whether it is your son's tunic or not?" And he recognized it and said, "It is my son's tunic. A wild beast has devoured him. Without doubt Joseph is torn to pieces"'* (Genesis 37:32–33).

Jesus (Psalm 22 – this is clearly a Messianic Psalm).

'For dogs have surrounded Me; the congregation of the wicked has enclosed Me. They pierced My hands and

My feet; I can count all My bones. They look and stare at Me ... Save Me from the lion's mouth and from the horns of the wild oxen!' (Psalm 22:16–17 & 21).

Psalm 22 was probably written around 1,000 BCE, four hundred years before crucifixion was first used by the Phoenicians for executing criminals.

8. God was with Joseph, as He was with Jesus.

Joseph *'The LORD was with Joseph, and he was a successful man; and he was in the house of his master the Egyptian. And his master saw that the LORD was with him and that the LORD made all he did to prosper in his hand. So Joseph found favour in his sight and served him'* (Genesis 39:2–4).

Jesus *'God was in Christ reconciling the world to Himself ... For He made Him who knew no sin to be sin for us, that we might become the righteousness of God in Him'* (2 Corinthians 5:19 & 21).

9. Joseph was tempted, as Jesus was tempted.

Joseph *"There is no one greater in this house than I, nor has he* [Joseph's master] *kept back anything from me but you, because you are his wife. How can I do this great wickedness and sin against God?"* (Genesis 39:9).

Jesus *'For we do not have a high priest who cannot sympathize with our weaknesses, but was in all points tempted as we are, yet was without sin'* (Hebrews 4:15).

10. **Joseph explained the dreams of Pharaoh's baker and his butler – as Jesus explained the mysteries of life and death.**

Because life and death are issues needing an explanation (as discussed in the Bible and within society), I have expanded my thoughts in this section to explain these juxtapositions between Joseph and Jesus.

Joseph In Genesis 40, we read of how Pharaoh's baker and his butler (they were in prison at the time) described for Joseph, dreams which had disturbed them. The two dreams (and Joseph's interpretation) are very significant when it comes to understanding Jesus, for the dreams speak of the provision of bread and wine, the two items Jesus used when teaching His disciples about Himself, and what He was about to do in laying down His life. Joseph's interpretation of the two dreams was that the baker would be executed in three days' time, but at the same time, the butler would be restored to his position of serving wine to Pharaoh – a type of resurrection.

Jesus The bread (baker) speaks to us of the body of Jesus. *'And He* [Jesus] *took bread, gave thanks and broke it, and gave it to them* [His disciples], *saying, "This is My body which is given for you; do this in remembrance of Me"'* (Luke 22:19).

When Jesus presented Himself to die, His life was taken from Him (as was the baker's life). In a similar way, our lives will eventually end; but for us there is hope.

The butler, who served wine to his master Pharaoh, was pardoned and restored. We, too (those who believe in Jesus), have been spared from the judgment of sin and have been restored to live and serve our Master, the Lord Jesus, because He poured out His life (His blood) for us. How did this happen? *'Likewise He also took the cup after supper, saying, "This cup is the new covenant in My blood, which is shed for you"'* (Luke 22:20).

When Jesus died, His blood was poured out as a sacrifice for sin (as the butler who had been forgiven, poured out wine for Pharaoh), for the life of Jesus was in His blood. The Bible confirms this: *'For the life of the flesh is in the blood'* (Leviticus 17:11).

Although all will one day experience a physical death (as happened to the baker and the body of Jesus), it is because the blood of Jesus is effective in pardoning all those who believe in Him from their sin, that the gift of everlasting life becomes effective – and immediately.

Pharaoh was bestowed with the power of life and death, and so he was able to restore his butler to serve wine in his hand. God's gift is to give eternal life to everyone who puts their hand in His hand. To understand what is clearly illustrated in this account of Pharaoh's baker and his butler, gives credence to what Jesus has done for those who seek to obey and to serve Him.

There is probably no clearer illustration in the whole of the Bible to demonstrate the consequences of sin and what the experience of sin's forgiveness is, other than Joseph's interpretation of the baker and butler's dreams. The significance of what happened to Pharaoh's baker and his butler was that it turned out just as Joseph had said. Yet the significance of the baker dying (bread) and the butler being set free (wine), is only fully realized in Jesus' willingness to present His body as a sacrifice for others, that His broken body and the shedding of His blood might become effective in the removing of sin.

Jesus was once asked to provide a sign to confirm He was the Christ, the Messiah. In His response Jesus said: *"An evil and adulterous generation seeks after a sign, and no sign will be given to it except the sign of the prophet Jonah. For as Jonah was three days and three nights in the belly of the great fish, so will the Son of Man be three days and three nights in the heart of the earth"* (Matthew 12:39–40).

What Jesus omitted to say (but what the Scribes and Pharisees should have known from their knowledge of their Scriptures), was that three days after their dreams, Pharaoh's chief baker was executed; he died. However, for Pharaoh's chief butler (after the three days), he was restored to serve wine in Pharaoh's Royal Court.

The three day period from when Pharaoh's chief baker and his chief butler dreamt their dreams, to when Joseph's interpretation of their dreams was implemented – confirming Joseph was in the place where God wanted him to be – mirrors perfectly the three days and the three nights that Jesus was in the tomb.

Christians (especially those who may face martyrdom for their faith), can be confident that although their bodies may be destroyed – for they are able to consider their bodies are already dead because of sin – nothing can rob them of the life of Jesus within them; for Jesus' blood cleanses from sin to enable restoration to Himself to take place.

In his letter to the new believers in Rome, Paul wrote: *'If Christ is in you, the body is dead because of sin, but the Spirit is life because of righteousness. But if the Spirit of Him who raised Jesus from the dead dwells in you, He who raised Christ from the dead will also give life to your mortal bodies through His Spirit who dwells in you'* (Romans 8:10–11).

When Joseph interpreted the dreams of his two fellow prisoners, it may well have been the first time Joseph became involved in a life and death situation. For the baker, for whatever reason he had been imprisoned, his dream indicated that in three days' time he would die. For Pharaoh's cup bearer (who also must have offended Pharaoh in some way), his dream was followed three days later by him being pardoned and restored to his position in Pharaoh's presence.

The more I have considered Joseph and his involvement with the baker and the cup bearer and their two dreams, the more I see of Jesus. Jesus is able to forgive and to restore us, and the means whereby this has become possible is the death of His body and His shed blood. And so we break bread to remember His broken body, and drink from the cup to remember His life's blood.

These two elements of the communion service are at the heart of the gospel, and we catch our first glimpse of them in a prison cell in Egypt; for Joseph was there to interpret the dreams of the baker and the butler – and he was inspired to do so for them and for everyone.

From when we first place our trust in Jesus, is when we can begin to experience being set free from our sin, for sin can so easily captivate our minds and our bodies.

Jesus said: *"Most assuredly, I say to you, whoever commits sin is a slave of sin. And a slave does not abide in the house forever, but a son abides forever. Therefore if the Son makes you free, you shall be free indeed"* (John 8:34–36).

11. **Joseph and Jesus were anointed by God with the Spirit of God.**

Joseph *'Pharaoh said to his servants, "Can we find such a one as this* [Joseph]*, a man in whom is the Spirit of God?"'* (Genesis 41:38).

Jesus *'And He* [Jesus] *was handed the book of the prophet Isaiah. And when He had opened the book, He* *found the place where it was written: "The Spirit of the Lord is upon Me, because He has anointed Me to preach the gospel to the poor; He has sent Me to heal the brokenhearted, to proclaim liberty to the captives and recovery of sight to the blind, to set at liberty those who are oppressed; to proclaim the acceptable year of the Lord."'*

'Then He closed the book, and gave it back to the attendant and sat down. And the eyes of all who were in the synagogue were fixed on Him. And He began to say to them, "Today this Scripture is fulfilled in your hearing"' (Luke 4:17–21).

12. **The people of Egypt and Jerusalem bowed down to Joseph and to Jesus.**

Joseph *'And he* [Pharaoh] *had him ride in the second chariot which he had; and they cried out before him, "Bow the knee!" So he set him over all the land of Egypt'* (Genesis 41:43).

Jesus *'The next day a great multitude that had come to the feast* [Passover] *when they heard that Jesus was coming to Jerusalem, took branches of palm trees and went out to meet Him and cried out: "Hosanna! Blessed is He who comes in the name of the LORD! The King of Israel!" Then Jesus, when He had found a young donkey,* [as opposed to a chariot] *sat on it; as it is written: "Fear not, daughter of Zion; behold, your King is coming, sitting on a donkey's colt"'* (John 12:12–15).

The apostle Paul wrote: *'Therefore God also has highly exalted Him and given Him the name which is above every name, that at the name of Jesus every knee should bow, of those in heaven, and those on earth, and those under the earth, and that every tongue should confess that Jesus Christ is Lord, to the glory of God the Father'* (Philippians 2:9–10).

13. **Joseph and Jesus were thirty years of age when they commenced their assignments.**

Joseph *'was thirty years old when he stood before Pharaoh King of Egypt. And he went out from the presence of Pharaoh ... throughout all the land of Egypt'* (Genesis. 41:46).

Jesus *'Now Jesus Himself began His ministry at about thirty years of age, being (as was supposed) the son of Joseph ... the son of God'* (Luke 3:23 & 38).

14. **Pharaoh told the people to do what Joseph said. At a wedding in Cana, Mary told the servants to do what Jesus said.**

Joseph *'So when all the land of Egypt was famished, the people cried to Pharaoh for bread. Then Pharaoh said to all the Egyptians, "Go to Joseph; whatever he says to you, do"'* (Genesis 41:55).

Jesus *'On the <u>third day</u> there was a wedding in Cana of Galilee, and the mother of Jesus was there. Now both*

Jesus and His disciples were invited to the wedding. And when they ran out of wine, the mother of Jesus said to Him, "They have no wine." Jesus said ... "Woman, what does your concern have to do with Me? My hour has not yet come." His mother said to the servants, "Whatever He says to you, do it"' (John 2:1–5).

The first miracle Jesus performed recalls a third day, the same length of time Joseph said would elapse following the interpretation of the baker and butler's two dreams. The miracle also involved wine – or the opposite, a lack of wine! When we consider Joseph's calling, it enables us to see why Joseph was sent to the Gentiles (Egypt), and why Jesus was sent to the Jews (Israel).

15. Joseph's brothers failed to recognize him. On the road to Emmaus, two of the disciples of Jesus failed to recognize Him.

Joseph *'Then Joseph could not restrain himself before all those who stood by him, and he cried out, "Make everyone go out from me!" So no one stood with him while Joseph made himself known to his brothers. Then Joseph said to his brothers, "I am Joseph: does my father still live?"'* (Genesis 45:1–3).

Jesus *'Now it came to pass, as He sat at the table with them, that He took bread, blessed it and broke it, and gave it to them. Then their eyes were opened and they knew Him: and He vanished from their sight'* (Luke 24:30–31).

Jesus later revealed Himself to all His disciples – the eleven, for Judas Iscariot was no longer with them. When Joseph eventually revealed himself to his brothers, there were eleven of them, for Joseph (like Jesus) was the twelfth; the one who had been missing! When we want to know more about Jesus and discover who He really is, it's not too difficult, for Jesus is portrayed (initially) so clearly in the life of Joseph.

16. **The final parallel – I'm sure there are others – concerns Joseph's name.**

Rachel, Jacob's second wife, bore for him two sons, and for the eldest of the two, Rachel named him Joseph (Genesis 30:24). Joseph is a Hebrew name and means: *'JEHOVAH will add, or increase'.*

When I discovered what Joseph's name means, it took me back to January 1964, when a visiting speaker at the church I attended in Cranleigh, Surrey, read from John's Gospel. The words that I still remember are those spoken by John the Baptist: *"He must increase, but I must decrease"* (John 3:30). Although at the time these seven words changed my life, I was not to know it would be fifty years before I learnt the meaning of Joseph's name, and that Joseph's name would find its fulfillment in the Lord Jesus: *'He must increase…'.*

Does this final analogy surpass the others? For myself, yes, for the Hebrew names of Joseph and Jesus conveys so much meaning. If Joseph's name means: *'JEHOVAH will Increase',* what is the meaning of Jesus' name? David Silver explains: *'In English, the word* [name] *Jesus does not convey a specific meaning; however in the Bible, Hebrew names carry a strong meaning. The word "Yeshua" means "SALVATION". In Isaiah 12:2 we read: Behold God is my salvation. In Hebrew, these words are given as "Hineh El Yeshua ti"'.*

God's Plan for Joseph and Jesus

In concluding this review of the lives of Joseph and Jesus, I know from personal experience that as we see Jesus in the closing chapters of Genesis, there can be no mistaking who He is. Like Joseph before Him, Jesus, as a child, had to go (briefly) down to Egypt, for He was sent by God to save lives; to give *'Life'* to others.

When Joseph's brothers sold Joseph to slave traders (distant cousins), then lied to their father that an animal may have killed him, knowing they had conspired to rid themselves of Joseph, it may appear Joseph's brothers had been cruel. Their reasoning was: *"Away with you, we refuse to bow down to you as you once dreamt!"* However, what happened to Joseph was not of their design. God knew Joseph needed to go down to Egypt to bring salvation, first to the Egyptians (Gentiles), then to Jacob's family (the Children of Israel), when famine struck their land.

When Joseph revealed himself to his brothers, he said to them: *"But now, do not therefore be grieved or angry with yourselves because you sold me here: for God sent me before you to preserve life. For these two years the famine has been in the land, and there are still five years in which there will be neither plowing nor harvesting. And God sent me before you to preserve a posterity for you in the earth, and to save your lives by a great deliverance. So now it was not you who sent me here, but God"* (Genesis 45:5–8).

For Jesus, God's plan mirrored that of Joseph – and vice-versa. It is true the first to put their trust in Jesus were mainly Jewish people, descendants of Abraham, Isaac, and Jacob, but during the last two thousand years, it has been mostly Gentiles who have trusted in Jesus, and it is He who has given them sustenance – His broken body (bread) and His poured-out blood (wine).

I believe a day is about to dawn when very many Jewish people will at last recognize Jesus as their Messiah – the *'Bread of Life'* – and He will rescue them from spiritual famine and give them life, as Joseph once gave corn to his brothers and their families for them to make bread.

****

On the next four pages there are fifteen questions which are based on this study. The suggested answers can be found on pages 216–217.

Study 2 Questions – Joseph and Jesus

1. In Genesis 30:22–24, we are told God opened Rachel's womb to enable Joseph to be born. Where in Mathew's Gospel do we read of God being involved in the conception of Jesus?

ANSWER: _____

2. The deaths of Joseph and Jesus were planned – but by who? (Genesis 37:20 & John 11:49–50).

ANSWER: _____

3. Joseph's brothers stripped him of his tunic (Genesis 37:23). When Jesus was crucified, who was involved in stripping Him of His tunic and where in the Psalms do we find a reference to this? (John 19:23–24).

ANSWER: _____

---

4. Joseph and Jesus were sold for financial gain. Who sold Jesus and for how much? Please give the reference. You will find it in Mathew's Gospel chapter 26.

ANSWER: _____

5. When Reuben went to look for Joseph (1), and certain women went to look for Jesus (2), where did Reuben look and where did the women look? (Genesis chapter 37 & Luke chapter 24).

ANSWER: _____

_____

6. When Joseph's brothers asked their father to identify Joseph's tunic, and what is written about Jesus, animals were said to have been involved. (1) What did Jacob say about his son? (Genesis 37:32–33). (2) What animals did the Psalmist include about Jesus? (Psalm 22:16–17 & 20–21).

ANSWER: _____

_____

7. (1) According to Genesis 39:2–4, who was with Joseph? (2) And according to 2 Corinthians 5:18–19, who was with Jesus?

ANSWER: _____

8. Joseph and Jesus were both tempted to do wrong – to sin against God. How were they tempted?

ANSWER: _____

_____

9. When Joseph was in prison he became closely involved with two other prisoners. The first was a baker who had baked bread for Pharaoh. The second was a butler who had served wine to Pharaoh. What are the two physical elements we partake of to remember Jesus?

ANSWER: _____

10. According to Genesis 41:38, what was so special about Joseph?

ANSWER: _____

_____

11. With reference to the last question, according to Luke 4:17–21, what passage of Scripture did Jesus quote and why did He do so?

ANSWER: _____

_____

12. When Joseph rode in Pharaoh's chariot, what did the people do? (Genesis 41:43). When Jesus entered Jerusalem riding on a donkey, what did the people do? (John 12:12–15).

ANSWER: _____

_____

13. How old was Joseph and how old was Jesus when they began their life's calling? (Genesis 41:46 & Luke 3:23).

ANSWER: _____

14. In Hebrew, Joseph's name means: *'JEHOVAH* [Yahweh] *will increase'.* What did John the Baptist say of Jesus? (John 3:30a)

ANSWER: _____

15. When Joseph made himself known to his brothers, all of them (eleven) were present (Genesis 45:1–4).

Eight days after His resurrection, Jesus made Himself known to His disciples. How many of Jesus' disciples would have been present? (John 20:24–31).

ANSWER: _____

****

STUDY 3 – THE ARK OF THE COVENANT

*'The first covenant had regulations for worship and it had its sanctuary, an earthly one. For a tent was constructed, of which the outer part was called the Holy Place, where the Lampstand and the table with the Bread of the Presence were; and beyond the second curtain was the Tent called the holy of holies. It had a golden altar of incense and the ark of the covenant, covered all over with gold. In the ark was a golden jar containing the manna, Aaron's staff which sprouted, and the stone tablets of the covenant. Above it were the cherubim of the Glory, and they overshadowed the place of reconciliation. **It is not possible now to speak of these things in detail**'* (Hebrews 9:1–5). (Emphasis added).

In his commentary on the book of Hebrews, author Tom Wright, says: *'Verse five is the sort of thing you say when you're giving a lecture and realise that, though there is much fascinating material you could include at this point, there isn't time for it, or perhaps the students are not ready for that level of complexity. We shall never know what this writer might have said about the altar, the ark, the urn, the cherubim and all the rest.'*

Is this true, will we never know? But equally important, is it right for us to know?

Many have a box for keeping various items; such as old coins, diaries, photographs, or an item from childhood. They may be of little value, but it is understandable why some people want to hang-on to their mementos.

God once told Moses to make a box. The reason He did so appears to be God wanted His people to learn certain lessons from the items He told His people to preserve. Why did God order Moses to do this? Surely, God must have had a very good reason for doing so? When God instructed Moses to make the tabernacle, each item was made for a purpose. The most important item, the Ark of the Covenant (a box which included a lid), was placed in the tabernacle's holy-of-holies – for it was here that God visited His people.

According to Exodus 37:1, *'Then Bezalel made the ark of acacia wood; two and half cubits was its length, a cubit and a half its width, and a cubit and a half its height.'* When completed, the Ark of the Covenant resembled an oblong box approximately one hundred and fifteen centimetres long, seventy centimetres wide, and seventy centimetres high. Within the ark, Moses placed the two stone tablets of the Ten Commandments, plus two other items. But why did God order Moses to do this?

In Hebrews nine, the writer recalls the symbolism of the tabernacle, and then he says that now is not the right time to describe some of the things he is writing about!

Why did the writer not explain what he was referring to? Can we speculate about something the writer does not explain, which for many has been, and remains still, an enigma?

God's instructions for the Ark of the Covenant and its purpose are very specific. The ark was a wooden box that included a lid, which was then overlaid with gold. The ark was used to safeguard the two stone tablets on which God inscribed the Ten Commandments, and it also featured in Israel's home and foreign affairs. In addition to the two stone tablets, what else did the ark contain? According to Hebrews 9:4, the writer lists three items that were placed in the Ark of the Covenant. The order of the three items is as follows.

1. **A golden pot of manna.** This was a container with a sample of the food God had provided for His people, the Children of Israel, while they were journeying in the Sinai desert.

2. **Aaron's rod.**

3. **The stone tablets of the Ten Commandments.**

The Golden Pot of Manna

After the Children of Israel's departure from Egypt, enthusiasm for a new way of life in a far-away country soon began to fade as they wished for death in Egypt, rather than die of starvation and thirst in the desert.

God responded by showing mercy. Each morning as the people rose, the first thing they did was to gather a small round substance which covered the ground around their tents. Referred to as: *'Manna'*, and tasting like wafers made with honey, it had the appearance of white coriander seeds (Exodus 16:31). Moses told the people to gather manna for each day, but on the sixth day, to gather sufficient manna for two days. On the Sabbath, the people were instructed not to go out and look for manna; however, some of the people went out on the Sabbath to look, but they found none. *'And the LORD said to Moses, "How long do you refuse to keep my commandments and my laws?"'* (Exodus 16:27–28).

The gift of manna was God's provision for the Children of Israel, for without it they and their children – those who entered the Promised Land – would have died in the wilderness. God's provision was so important He instructed Moses to save a sample of the manna and for it to be kept as a witness for future generations. The manna was to be kept in a golden pot and placed before the testimony. According to Hebrews, it was placed in the Ark of the Covenant. Why did God instruct Moses to do this? The pot of manna was to act as a token to show that God was able to provide for Israel's needs.

Aaron's Rod

It is clear from the book of Numbers (chapters 16 & 17) that not everyone was pleased with God's choice of

Moses and Aaron as His appointed representatives. Korah, a Levite, wanted power – and Korah was not alone. Dathan and Abiram, the sons of Eliab, joined forces with him and together they formed an alliance of two hundred and fifty leaders from among the people. Their plan was to stage a political coup by confronting Moses and Aaron directly. Speaking on behalf of the rebels, Korah said to Moses and Aaron: *"You, take too much upon yourselves, for all the congregation is holy, every one of them, and the Lord is among them. Why then do you exalt yourselves above the assembly of the Lord?"* (Numbers 16:3). Sounds plausible, doesn't it? *"Moses, it's now time for you and your brother to share power – or step aside!"* I can imagine Korah saying to Moses and Aaron: *"Moses, what you are doing is not democratic; a coalition leadership/government is what the people need – and we would like to be a part of it!"*

To make their demand seem reasonable, one which had widespread support, Korah described their position as one that included all the Children of Israel. *'All the congregation is holy, every one of them, and the Lord is among them'* – therefore, what we are demanding must be right in the Lord's sight, suggested Korah!

Moses must have been shocked. *"Tell me Aaron, this is not happening!"* Moses was so shocked he fell on his face (verse 4). There was rebellion in the camp and Moses knew this was a serious offence; not against himself and his brother Aaron, but against God.

Numbers chapter sixteen describes Korah's rebellion and its outcome. Infuriated that Korah and his friends should challenge His choice of Moses and Aaron as His representatives, God opened the ground beneath Korah and he and the rest of the conspirators, together with their families, perished (verses 31–33).

Following the punishment of Korah and those who supported him, *'On the next day all the congregation of the children of Israel complained against Moses and Aaron saying, "You have killed the people of the Lord"'* (Numbers 16:41)!

God, understandably, was angry (righteous anger), and so He descended and His glory covered the tabernacle. God told Moses and Aaron He was about to consume the entire congregation of the Children of Israel! Once again Moses fell on his face, for he knew he had to act swiftly if he was to save some of the people from God's judgement.

Moses told Aaron to take fire from the altar and to go to the congregation of the people to make atonement – and to do so immediately, as the plague had begun and people were dying. With his censer in his hand, Aaron moved quickly among the living and the dead until gradually the plague was checked; but not before it had taken its toll. By the time Aaron had passed through the camp and returned to Moses at the door of tabernacle, 14,700 people had died (Numbers 16:46–50).

Two rebellions in two days was two too many, and so God told Moses to prepare for a demonstration of His authority. Moses was ordered to instruct the leaders of the twelve tribes of Israel to each submit a rod, first having carved their names on their rods. Once they had done this, Moses placed the rods before the tabernacle. The rods were to be used to show who God had selected as His representative(s): Aaron (and Moses), or others; and the result would have to be passed down from one generation to the next. Having done as God had instructed him, Moses then retired to his tent to await the outcome of what theocracy would decide.

The next morning (Numbers 17:8), Moses went into the tabernacle to see if anything unusual had taken place. Moses saw that one of the rods had budded; it had produced blossoms and ripe almonds. The rod which had budded had Aaron's name on it and was the proof Moses needed to show that God had chosen Aaron as His representative; to have authority as God's servant over God's people, and for Aaron to do so in God's presence in the tabernacle (and in particular in the holy-of-holies on the Day of Atonement).

Having confirmed Aaron was His servant, God ordered Moses to preserve Aaron's rod as a token for future generations. The reason was because God's people must learn to respect God's choice of those He wishes to carry out His instructions, regardless of status. Thus Aaron's rod was placed in the Ark of the Covenant.

The Stone Tablets of the Ten Commandments

The two stone tablets which God gave to Moses had inscribed on them the Ten Commandments, and they speak to us of direction; what God requires of us if we are to have a relationship with Him and with each other – and without conflict. The Ten Commandments are…

1. **You shall have no other gods before Me.**

2. **You shall not make for yourself any graven image.**

3. **You shall not take the name of God in vain.**

4. **Remember the Sabbath day – to keep it holy.**

5. **Honour your father and your mother.**

6. **You shall not kill (murder).**

7. **You shall not commit adultery.**

8. **You shall not steal.**

9. **You shall not bear false witness.**

10. **You shall not covet your neighbour's house.**

God's reason for providing us with instructions about how we should live our lives is important, for without His guidance there would be chaos. There are many Scriptures confirming this, for example: *'I will instruct you and teach you in the way you should go; I will guide you with My eye'* (Psalm 32:8).

And in Deuteronomy: *"Every commandment which I command you today you must be careful to observe, that you may live and multiply, and go in and possess the land of which the Lord swore to your fathers. And you shall remember that the Lord your God led you all the way these forty years in the wilderness, to humble you and test you, to know what was in your heart, whether you would keep His commandments or not. So He humbled you, allowed you to hunger, and fed you with manna which you did not know nor did your fathers know, that He might make you know that man shall not live by bread alone; but man lives by every word that proceeds from the mouth of the Lord. Your garments did not wear out on you, nor did your foot swell these forty years. You should know in your heart that as a man chastens his son, so the Lord your God chastens you. Therefore you shall keep the commandments of the Lord your God, to walk in His ways and to fear Him"* (Deuteronomy 8:1–6).

The last part of this section in Deuteronomy is similar to Hebrews 12:9–10. *'Furthermore, we have had human fathers who corrected us, and we paid them respect. Shall we not much more readily be in subjection to the Father of spirits and live? For they indeed for a few days chastened us as seemed best to them, but He for our profit, that we may be partakers of His holiness.'* God's plan is for us is to participate in His holiness. First, however, we must accept the need for obedience.

Psalm 119 (this Psalm is illustrated in many Bibles with the letters of the Hebrew alphabet), is time-less when it comes to learning the importance of obedience. *'Teach me, O Lord, the way of your statutes, and I shall keep it to the end. Give me understanding, and I shall keep Your law; indeed, I shall observe it with my whole heart. Make me walk in the path of Your commandments, for I delight in it. Incline my heart to Your testimonies, and not to covetousness. Turn away my eyes from looking at worthless things, and revive me in Your way'* (Psalm 119:33–37).

The Order of the Three Items Placed within the Ark of the Covenant – are they a 'Mirror Image'?

The way the three items are described in Hebrews 9:4, is, I believe, important; however, the order is the reverse of what I would have expected, given the importance of each of the three items. I was puzzled, that is until I saw the order as a perfect mirror image.

In John's Gospel, nine chapters are devoted to the final day Jesus spent with His disciples, the three days of His trial, crucifixion, death, and resurrection, and during the forty days before He was taken up (Acts 1:9). During this time, Jesus spoke to His disciples mainly about the Kingdom of God and how the Holy Spirit would help them in their future relationship with Him.

At His first coming, Jesus marked a transition from the old traditions of knowing God, to a new and living way, based on His teachings, explaining who He was and what He would leave behind as His legacy. Therefore, did Jesus share with His disciples, anything which may have had a connection to the Ark of the Covenant? The answer, I suggest, is in the contents of the Ark of the Covenant and what these three items represented.

With His remaining hours ebbing away, Jesus said to His disciples that within His Father's house were many mansions, and that He was going to prepare a place for them. Jesus then explained the relationship He had with His Father and what they would experience once He had left them. At the time when Jesus and His disciples were preparing for the annual Passover celebration, was Jesus thinking about Israel's high-priest when, on the Day of Atonement, he would enter the holy-of-holies in the temple and sprinkle animal blood on the mercy seat – the place where atonement for sin was to take place? The mercy seat was the covering of Israel's Ark of the Covenant; and within the ark was Aaron's pot of manna, his rod, and the two tablets of stone on which God had inscribed the Ten Commandments. As we have seen, each of these items represented three things.

1. **The manna** – God's provision for His people.

2. **Aaron's rod** – God's authority.

3. **The Ten Commandments** – God's instructions for teaching His people how they should live their lives.

This is the setting where I became aware of a mirror image. Jesus said to His disciples that they could only come to the Father through Him; however, prior to this, Jesus had informed them of three important truths concerning Himself: *"I am the way, the truth and the life"* (John 14:6a). The order is the reverse of what is given in Hebrews 9:4, but this is how Jesus described this aspect of His life and ministry. Jesus is the *'Way'* – God's direction for our lives. Jesus is the *'Truth'* – God's authority. Jesus is the *'Life'* – God's provision.

"I am the Way" Indicates Direction

After Jesus had said: *"I am the way,"* He said: *"No one comes to the Father except through Me"* (John 14:6b). Clearly, Jesus was saying – I am the way to the Father.

Prior to the coming of Jesus, intimacy with God was reserved for Israel's high priest when he entered the holy-of-holies, the location for the Ark of the Covenant. There was only one access by which the high priest could approach God, through the veil – and on only one day a year, the Day of Atonement. *'Therefore brethren, having boldness to enter the Holiest by the blood of Jesus, by a new and living way which He consecrated for us, through the veil, that is His flesh, and having a high priest over the house of God, let us draw near with a true heart in full assurance of faith, having our hearts sprinkled from an evil conscience and our bodies washed with pure water'* (Hebrews 10:19–22).

"I am the Truth" Indicates Authority

When Pilate questioned Jesus, he asked Him: *"Are you a king then?"* Jesus answered Pilate: *"You say rightly that I am a king. For this cause I was born and for this cause I have come into the world, that I should bear witness to the truth. Everyone who is of the truth hears my voice"* (John 18:37–38). Pilate listened to what Jesus had to say to him and then asked Him: *"What is truth?"* Pilate then spoke to those who were demanding His crucifixion and said to them: *"I find no fault in Him."* (Pilate said this of Jesus, three times).

The public trial of Jesus was as decisive in establishing who represented God, as when Moses placed Aaron's rod before God, for God to show who He had chosen; Aaron, or those who wanted Aaron's job. Aaron's rod, made of wood, confirmed his appointment as God's representative. At Calvary, a wooden cross became the means whereby God confirmed His appointment of Jesus as His final representative – Jesus who now stands before God with authority and on our behalf.

When Pilate asked Jesus, *"What is truth?"* he was looking *'Truth'* – the authority of God – straight in the eye. He then placed a notice on the cross above Jesus: *'JESUS OF NAZARETH, KING OF THE JEWS'* (John 19:19). Speaking of Himself, Jesus had earlier said: *"Therefore My Father loves Me, because I lay down My life that I may take it again. No one takes it from Me, but I lay it down and I have power to take it again. This command* [authority] *I have received from My Father"* (John 10:17–18). (Note: The Jews did not kill Jesus).

When writing prophetically, Isaiah described Jesus' authority using terms that Moses and Aaron, centuries earlier, would have been familiar with. *'There shall come forth a Rod from the stem of Jesse. And a Branch shall grow out of his roots. The Spirit of the Lord shall rest upon Him, the Spirit of wisdom and understanding, the Spirit of counsel and might, the Spirit of knowledge and of the fear of the Lord'* (Isaiah 11:1–2).

Jeremiah also wrote using similar words: *'"Behold, the days are coming" says the Lord, "That I will raise to David a Branch of righteousness; a King shall reign and prosper, and execute judgment and righteousness in the earth. In His days Judah will be saved, and Israel will dwell safely. Now this is His name* [as with Aaron's name on his rod] *by which He will be called: 'THE LORD OUR RIGHTEOUSNESS'"'* (Jeremiah 23:5–6).

After His resurrection, Jesus said to His disciples: *"All authority is given to Me in heaven and on earth. Go therefore and make disciples of all nations, baptising them in the name of the Father and of the Son and of the Holy Spirit, teaching them to observe all things that I have commanded you; and lo, I am with you always, even to the end of the age"* (Matthew 28:18–20). Jesus was saying – I have authority to do My Father's will.

"I am the Life" Indicates Provision

The following is taken (in sections) from John 6:30–51.

'Therefore they [the Jews] *said to Him* [Jesus]*: "What sign will you perform then, that we may see it and believe you? What work will you do? Our fathers ate manna in the desert: as it is written: 'He gave them bread from heaven to eat.'"'*

'Jesus answered and said to them, "Most assuredly, I say to you, Moses did not give you the bread from heaven, but My Father gives you the true bread from heaven. For the bread of God is He who comes down from heaven and gives life to the world." Then they said to Him, "Lord give us this bread always." Jesus said to them, "I am the bread of life. He who comes to Me shall never hunger and he who believes in Me shall never thirst ... For I have come down from heaven, not to do my own will, but the will of Him who sent me ... And this is the will of Him who sent Me, that everyone who sees the Son and believes in Him may have everlasting life; and I will raise him up at the last day."'

'"I am the bread of life. Your fathers ate the manna in the wilderness and are dead. This is the bread which comes down from heaven that one may eat of it and not die. I am the living bread which came down from heaven. If anyone eats of this bread, he will live forever and the bread that I shall give is My flesh, which I give for the life of the world."'

Jesus surrendered His entitlement to an earthly life that He might become the giver of God's provision; that we may have *'Life'* and gain access to the inheritance He has gone to prepare for those who love Him.

Additional Evidence

There are numerous illustrations in the Old Testament which refers to Jesus, but one in particular that refers to these three-fold attributes of Himself: *"I am the way, the truth, and the life."*

We saw in study two how Joseph's name means: *'JEHOVAH will add, or increase'*, and how Joseph was aware of God's leading when he was taken down to Egypt; which matched some of the truths that Jesus taught His disciples concerning Himself.

In Genesis 45:1–8, we read of what Joseph said to his brothers concerning what had taken place in his life.

1. *"It was not you who sent me down to Egypt, but God."* – Direction.

2. *"God has made me a father to Pharaoh, and lord of all his house, and a ruler throughout all the land of Egypt."* – Authority.

3. This happened to Joseph because: *"God sent me before you to preserve a posterity for you in the earth and to save your lives by a great deliverance."* – Provision.

For Jacob's family, because Joseph was called by God to become their saviour – from hunger and from death – Joseph was a type of Jesus, *'The way, the truth, and the life'*. (Genesis 45:1–8).

As we consider the golden pot of manna (provision), Aaron's rod which budded (authority) and the two tablets of stone of the Ten Commandments (direction) we can learn so much about Jesus, His role in the lives of the Hebrew people, His Church, and in our individual lives also.

Jesus the *'Way'* is the One we must focus on if we are to have fellowship with God. Direction is what the Torah (the first five books of the Bible), is mostly about. Jesus said He did not come to abolish the law, but to fulfil it. In the upper room when Jesus was facing the certainty of His death, He said to His disciples: *"If you love Me, keep My commandments"* (John 14:15). This is the same message that Samuel reminded King Saul he should have observed: *"Behold, to obey is better than sacrifice"* (1 Samuel 15:22).

The importance of direction is why the two tablets of stone on which the Ten Commandments were inscribed, were placed in the Ark of the Covenant. Jesus is the *'Way'* – God's direction for us.

Jesus the *'Truth'* indicates Jesus was granted authority (God's authority). Aaron's rod which budded spoke to the Children of Israel about who God had chosen with regard to leadership and authority. When the Children of Israel rebelled, it was God who caused Aaron's rod to bud, to flower and to fruit, as a sign of God's choice in choosing Aaron (and Moses) as His representative(s).

Today, we are called to believe that Jesus is indeed God's chosen one, and therefore we can take His words, His death, His resurrection, and His ascension, as proof of His divine appointment to exercise authority over His people; for truth can never be changed. God's truth will never become out-of-date. Jesus is the *'Truth'* – God's chosen authority for us.

Jesus the *'Life'* reminds us He is able to equip us with all we need, both in this life and in the life to come. Did Jesus not say concerning Himself: *"I am the Bread of Life"* (John 6:48)? The manna in the wilderness and the golden pot of manna which was placed in the Ark of the Covenant, anticipated the coming of Jesus who would give *'Life'* to those who would believe in Him.

The order Jesus placed on these three attributes of Himself is the reverse of what is written in Hebrews 9:4, which gives details of the Ark of the Covenant and its contents. Jesus is the perfect *'Mirror Image'* of the Ark of the Covenant, its lid (God's mercy), and its contents.

Tracking the Ark

Charles Foster, a British explorer, has spent much time, finance and effort in trying to locate the original Ark of the Covenant. In his book, *'Tracking the Ark'*, Foster writes: *'I don't know what the ark is about, and I know less now than I ever did. I have never met anyone who has got any devotional mileage from the ark.'* Foster continues by saying: *'I despair wholly of getting any systematic theology of the ark.'* Although Foster raises questions about the purpose of the ark, Foster does conclude: *'The importance of the Exodus ark lay not in what was on the outside, but in what was on the inside and who could be met with on the lid.'*

Foster's conclusion about the Ark of the Covenant and its contents, demonstrates that he at least understands their significance, even though as he admits, the Ark of the Covenant remains (for him) a mystery.

The apostle Paul was also aware of taking into account a greater four dimensional view of the life and ministry of Jesus, when he wrote to the believers in Ephesus: *'May Christ dwell in your hearts through faith; and that you being rooted and grounded in love, may be able to comprehend with all the saints what is the breadth and length and height and depth – and to know the love of Christ which surpasses knowledge; that you may be filled with all the fullness of God'* (Ephesians 3:17–19).

The next time you read about or consider Israel's Ark of the Covenant, remember not only its breadth, its length and its height, but also remember its depth. Take a look inside, observe its contents, and discover who Jesus is.

If one-day someone claims to have discovered the Ark of the Covenant; then beware, it may cause more problems than it will solve! Yes, it will confirm the biblical narrative, but for those who believe in Jesus, there is no longer a need for the Ark of the Covenant, or for its replacement, for it would become a distraction.

When assessing the purpose of the Ark of the Covenant (why it was made), I can think of only one other object mentioned in Scripture that may have been of a similar size, shape, and made of similar material (wood) that surpassed the Ark of the Covenant (which was placed in the holy-of-holies). Could not the manger in which Mary placed her new-born Son, be seen as an alternative for the Ark of the Covenant; for was not the manger in Bethlehem representative of that ark?

The only place in Scripture where it lists specifically the contents of the Ark of the Covenant is in Hebrews chapter nine, verses 4–5. Regarding the manger, there was only one item the manger lacked – the mercy seat, the covering for the ark. Mary, however, knowing it was unthinkable for her to place Jesus in a manger without some form of covering, wrapped her new-born Son in swaddling cloths (as Aaron would have clothed himself in a simple linen garment before entering the holy-of-holies on the Day of Atonement, the room where the Ark of the Covenant was placed). Later in His life, Jesus taught His disciples, saying: *'I am the way, the truth, and the life'* (God's way, God's truth and God's life).

Jesus, I believe, is the most logical fulfilment of the Ark of the Covenant and its contents; why God told Moses the items must be preserved as indicators.

Under the Old Covenant system of approaching God, only one man, Israel's high priest, could enter fully into God's presence, and on only one day a year, the Day of Atonement.

Under the New Covenant system, because Jesus is:

1. **The Way – direction to God**

2. **The Truth – the appointed authority of God**

3. **The Life – the provision of God…**

…everyone can now enter God's presence. The reason is because Jesus is our High Priest, interceding on our behalf. However, for us to enter fully into His presence, we should take note of the following injunction:

'If we say that we have no sin, we deceive ourselves and the truth is not in us. If we confess our sins, He is faithful and just to forgive us our sins and to cleanse us from all unrighteousness. If we say that we have not sinned, we make Him a liar, and His word is not in us' (1 John 1:8–10).

****

FOOTNOTE TO AARON'S ROD

It was not until after I had returned from Moldova that I began to consider a deeper meaning of Aaron's rod. As we have learnt from this study, it is in Numbers we read of how Aaron's rod was placed before the *'Testimony'* (the Ten Commandments that were placed in the Ark of the Covenant – Exodus 40:20 & Numbers 17:4). Prior to this, we read: *'The LORD spoke to Moses saying: "And you shall write Aaron's name on the rod of Levi. For there shall be one rod for the head of each father's house"'* (verses 1 and 3). The Levites were the priests who ministered on behalf of the people.

Why was it important Aaron's *name* was written on his rod? From the book of Numbers, we know the outcome of the test. Overnight, Aaron's rod sprang into life and became fruitful, rather than the rods of those who complained and found fault with Aaron (and with God).

Thus we have Aaron's rod with his name on it – living, with buds, blossom and fruit. Without a doubt, it was a most remarkable miracle, *"a sign against the rebels that you may put their complaints away from Me, lest they die"* (Numbers 17:10), said the LORD to Moses.

Consider now the arrest and the trial of Jesus, and what at the time must have appeared to His mother and His disciples as a serious miscarriage of justice – but was it?

After the mock-trial of Jesus, the chief priests and the officers appealed to Pilate, *"Crucify Him, crucify Him!"* (John 19:6). Pilate, appointed by Caesar as the ruler of Jerusalem (the city where God had placed His *'Name'* – 2 Chronicles 6:6), knowing Jesus had not committed any crime but unable to placate His accusers, Pilate then authorized Jesus to be crucified. Remarkably, it seems, Pilate had a sudden rush of inspiration – he ordered a sign to be fixed to the cross of Jesus for the benefit of those who wanted to rid themselves of Him (as Joseph's brothers had wanted to rid themselves of Joseph).

The sign did not list the crimes of Jesus – for there were none – but written on the sign were these words: *'JESUS OF NAZARETH, THE KING OF THE JEWS'* (John 19:19). The sign gave His name and His title. Had he wanted to be a little more accurate, Pilate might have written: *'JESUS OF NAZARETH, KING OF KINGS AND LORD OF LORDS'* (Revelation 19:16) but had he done so, he would probably have been court-marshaled. It was left to a Roman centurion to add the final epitaph, the one that was really important: *"Truly this Man was the Son of God"* (Mark 15:39).

Is it not striking as Aaron wrote his name on his rod, so Pilate wrote the name of Jesus and fixed it to His cross? Although Aaron had his faults, Aaron was still God's representative, and it was essential that Aaron was able to pre-figure what God would eventually do. The reason was because what happened to Aaron's rod – it became fruitful – pre-figured what would happen centuries later, when Pilate fixed the name of Jesus as a sign to His cross. In the same way as Aaron's rod had budded and became fruitful, so the wooden cross of Jesus has been the means whereby many have been saved as they have come to an understanding of the gospel.

Shortly before He died, Jesus said to His disciples: *"By this is My Father glorified, that you bear much fruit; so you will be My disciples"* (John 15:8). And in verse 16: *"You did not choose Me, but I chose you and appointed you that you should go and bear fruit, and that your fruit should remain, that whatever you ask the Father in My name He may give you."* The terminology of fruitfulness is how Jesus described the future work of His disciples, after He died on the cross – not unlike the fruit that appeared on Aaron's rod.

Until I embarked on the final preparation for this book, the above had not occurred to me; not in the way I have described. But is this not the allure of the foundations of the Christian faith? There is just so much about Jesus in the New Testament that is pre-figured in the Old. And if at times the imagery appears vague, the Holy Spirit is available to assist us.

****

On the next four pages there are fifteen questions which are based on this study. The suggested answers can be found on pages 218–219.

Study 3 Questions – The Ark of the Covenant

1. In Hebrews 9:4, we read that within the Ark of the Covenant was a pot containing a sample of the manna God provided for His people (Exodus 16), Aaron's rod which budded (Numbers 16 & 17), and the two tablets of stone on which God inscribed the Ten Commandments (Exodus 34). The writer says: *'It is not possible to speak of these things in detail'.* Do you think we should study the deeper meaning of these three items?

ANSWER: _____

2. It was God who told Moses to make the Ark of the Covenant. Once it was made, where it placed? (Exodus 26:34).

ANSWER: _____

3. According to Hebrews 9:4, the first item that is described as being placed in the Ark of the Covenant was a jar of manna. What did this sample of manna represent? (Exodus 16).

ANSWER: _____

4. The next item was Aaron's rod. What did Aaron's rod represent? (Numbers 16 & 17).

ANSWER: _____

5. The third item was the stone tablets on which God wrote the Ten Commandments (Exodus 34). What did the commandments represent?

ANSWER: _____

_____

6. Jesus said: *"I am the way, the truth and the life. No one comes to the Father except through Me."* (John 14:6). If we take this statement of Jesus, and consider the three items that were placed in the Ark of the Covenant, which of these three items represents Jesus as being *'The Way'*?

ANSWER: _____

7. Bearing in mind the Ark of the Covenant was placed within the holy-of-holies and Israel's high priest could only enter the holy-of-holies once a year – on the Day of Atonement – how can we draw near to God? (Hebrews 10:19–22).

ANSWER: _____

_____

8. Which of these three items represents Jesus as being *'The Truth'*?

ANSWER: _____

9. When Jesus was standing before Pilate, Jesus said to him: *"Everyone who is of the truth hears My voice."* Pilate then asked Jesus: *"What is truth?"* Pilate then said to the accusers of Jesus: *"I find no fault in Him at all."* How many times did Pilate say Jesus was innocent of any crime or wrongdoing? (John 18 & 19).

ANSWER: _____

10. Which of the three items represents Jesus as being *'The Life'*?

ANSWER: _____

11. Jesus was once asked: *"What sign will you perform then, that we may see it and believe you?"* In His reply Jesus said: *"For the bread of God..."* Complete this statement (John 6:33 & 35).

ANSWER: _____

_____

_____

_____

12. In study two we saw that Joseph mirrored the person of Jesus in various ways; including what Jesus said: *"I am the way, the truth and the life."* (Direction, Authority and Provision). In Genesis we read of when Joseph made himself known to his brothers. Who was responsible for sending Joseph to Egypt? (Genesis 45:5 & 7).

ANSWER: _____

13. Who was responsible for making Joseph a ruler with authority throughout all the land of Egypt? (Genesis 45:8).

ANSWER: _____

14. What was the real reason Joseph was sent down to Egypt – in order for him to do what? (Genesis 45:9–11).

ANSWER: _____

15. The Ark of the Covenant is described as having breadth, length and height. What is the fourth dimension of the ark and why is this so important? (Ephesians 3:17–19).

ANSWER: _____

_____

****

STUDY 4 – THE TABERNACLE

For those who may be averse to numerology, the study of numbers, although at times it can be hard work, it can also be to our advantage. When numbers appear in the Bible they frequently add meaning to the text, for it is a Hebrew method of teaching biblical truth. For example, seven may indicate design and might be used to reveal aspects of *'Spiritual Perfection'*. Thus (in the Bible) we discover, the *'Seven days of creation; the Seven days of the Feast of Unleavened Bread; the Seven Sabbaths from the Feast of Firstfruits to the Feast of Weeks; and the Seven days of the Feast of Tabernacles'*. In Scripture numbers are educationally important when it comes to understanding biblical truth; particularly so regarding our relationship with God and His Son, the Lord Jesus.

Ten is another important number and often appears in Scripture to reveal aspects of the *'Perfection of Divine Order'*. In his very helpful book, *'Number in Scripture'*, E. W. Bullinger explains the true significance of ten: *'It implies nothing is wanting; that the number and order are perfect; that the whole cycle is complete.'*

The Ten Commandments which God gave to Moses are perhaps the most well-known example of ten being the perfection of divine order, for they were designed to teach men and women how to live in harmony with God and with each other – and to do so without conflict.

A number of years ago, my wife and I attended a conference near Manchester, England, and David Davis from the Mount Carmel Fellowship in Israel was one of the speakers. Encouraged by his ministry, we purchased David's book, *'The Elijah Legacy'*, and was introduced to *'The Methodology on Midrash'*. David explains:

'There is an ancient Jewish concept of understanding biblical prophecy called Midrash. The word comes from a root which means, 'To Search'. Hebrew writers and commentators understood and applied four basic modes of interpretation to Scripture and biblical prophecy. These include,'

1. **Simple** *'Plain, literal sense of the text.'*

2. **Hint** *'A word, phrase, or some other element in the text that hints at things of which the writer was not aware, which is not conveyed by the simple meaning.'*

3. **Search** *'An allegorical application of the text.'*

4. **Secret** *'A hidden meaning.'*

'Midrash is a Hebrew methodology of understanding prophecy. Prophecy is not only a specific or simple prediction, but also contains 'Hints' and a 'Search' for deeper meaning. Sometimes, there can be a 'Secret' meaning. Therefore there are often multiple fulfillments [or layers] of a single prophecy.'

The Tabernacle – Israel's Tent of Meeting

Examples of *'Midrash'* abound in Scripture and perhaps none more so than in the tabernacle made by Moses for the Children of Israel. The tabernacle, of course, was not man's invention or his idea of how to approach God. Everything about the tabernacle was designed by God. Therefore, it should not surprise us there may be up to four layers of meaning associated with the tabernacle's various items and how they were arranged. I believe it is true to say that the most important man-made object in the whole of human creation was Israel's tabernacle of meeting, for it was where the Children of Israel were able to draw near to God and to receive instructions from Him.

The tabernacle was also the place where the Children of Israel received forgiveness for their wrongdoing. The same is true of Jesus, for Jesus has taught us how we should live and how we can approach Him and receive His forgiveness. The apostle John reminds us that Jesus came to tabernacle among us (John 1:14).

Mount Sinai

After the Children of Israel had left Egypt (the Exodus), they journeyed south through the Wilderness of Sinai and three months later arrived at Mount Sinai (Exodus 19:1). It was here God gave Moses detailed instructions about how the tabernacle was to be made and what it was to be used for.

Additionally, God not only designed the tabernacle, He designed the plan for our salvation, which culminated in the sending of His Son. Therefore, in this study, I will be concentrating on the seventeen major items (7 + 10) included in Israel's tabernacle.

It has been said: *'The sum of an object is its parts'*, and this is particularly true of Israel's tabernacle. The beauty of the tabernacle is it enables us to see Jesus – and in a way that describes who He is and why He came.

(1) **The Curtain of the Outer Court** formed the outer perimeter of the tabernacle and included the fixtures and fittings used to support the curtain. The curtain was one hundred cubits long, fifty cubits wide (46 x 23 meters), and was made from fine white linen. When white linen is referred to in the Bible, it is usually associated with righteousness. The prophet Jeremiah wrote: *'Now this is His name by which He will be called: "THE LORD OUR RIGHTEOUSNESS"'* (Jeremiah 23:6).

The curtain represented the name and the righteousness of God in the midst of His people. Whenever we draw near to God, as the Children of Israel drew near to the tabernacle, we do not come in our own righteousness, but we come to Him in the righteousness of His Son, the Lord Jesus. For men and women to live a godly and holy life, they must be: *'In Christ Jesus, who became for us wisdom from God – and righteousness and sanctification and redemption'* (1 Corinthians 1:30).

(2) **The Gate** of the tabernacle was where the priests and the people, who brought their offerings to God, entered the outer court. Known as: *'The Eastern Gate'*, the gate measured five cubits high and twenty cubits wide (2.3 x 9.2 meters).

In Hebrew, five indicates grace; twenty is the number of expectancy. When we come to God in faith and repentance, grace and expectancy must co-exist. *'For by grace you have been saved through faith, and that not of yourselves; it is the gift of God'* (Ephesians 2:8). Grace opens the door for us to enter God's presence; expectancy is the fruit of faith. In Hebrews chapter four we find written: *'Let us therefore come boldly to the throne of grace, that we may obtain mercy and find grace to help in time of need'* (Hebrews 4:16).

The eastern gate is also an example of grace – it was positioned on the east side of the tabernacle. Camped opposite was the tribe of Judah, and Judah's emblem was a lion. *'But one of the elders said to me, "Do not weep. Behold, the Lion of the tribe of Judah, the Root of David, has prevailed to open the scroll and to loose its seven seals"'* (Revelation 5:5). Opening the scroll is like opening a gate (or door).

Jesus said: *"Most assuredly, I say to you, I am the door of the sheep"* (John 10:7). Jesus also said: *"I am the door. If anyone enters by Me, he will be saved, and will go in and out and find pasture"* (John 10:9).

Jacob also knew the wonder of being in God's presence, for when he awoke he said: *"Surely the Lord is in this place, and I did not know it."* Jacob was afraid, and so his response was: *"How awesome is this place! This is none other than the house of God, and this is the gate of heaven!"* (Genesis 28:16–17).

Although for those who entered the tabernacle its gate was on its east side, they would have been facing west. In Ezekiel, we read of certain men who positioned themselves at the door of the temple with their backs to the door. Why was this so wrong? It was because they were facing east and were worshipping the sun toward the east (Ezekiel 8:16). Facing the sun, rather than God's Son, is not the right way to worship God.

(3) **The Altar of Burnt Offerings** (or Brazen Altar) was used for the burnt offerings the priests offered to God on behalf of the people. There were only two items in the tabernacle that are referred to as being: *'Most Holy'*, the brazen and golden altars. The brazen altar was a forerunner to the cross on which Jesus died; both involved suffering, both involved death, and each provided a way for God's people to draw near to Him.

Whenever the brazen altar was moved, it was always covered with a scarlet cloth (Numbers 4:13). Roman soldiers, too, dressed Jesus in a scarlet robe and mocked Him before leading Him out to be crucified. Scarlet in the Bible denotes suffering, but it was not the brazen altar or the cross on which Jesus died that removes sin. It was the sacrifice that was placed on the brazen altar, and Jesus who died on the cross, that removes sin.

(4) **The Sacrifice** – the shedding of blood, because *'the life of the flesh is in the blood'* (Leviticus 17:11 & Deuteronomy 12:23) – was a substitute that died for the forgiveness of sin. On the Day of Atonement, two male goats were selected. One was killed and its blood became the sin offering. For the other goat – known as the *'Scapegoat'* — the priests laid their hands on its head and confessed over it the sins of the people before it was led into the wilderness by *'A suitable man'* and set free (Leviticus 16:21).

In our own wilderness of sin – whatever sin or wherever that wilderness may have taken us – Jesus became for us a substitute sacrifice. The purity of His sinless life and His shed blood can cleanse us from all sin (1 John 1:7). Therefore, the exchange of His sin-free life for our sinful life is what makes us God's people.

(5) **The Bronze Laver** – positioned in the outer court – was used by the priests to wash their hands and feet before entering the tent of meeting. When Jesus was preparing to enter *'the Most Holy Place once for all'* with His own blood (Hebrews 9:12), there was no need for Him to wash His hands or His feet – soon to become stained with His blood – however, Jesus took a basin (a type of laver) to wash the feet of His disciples.

Peter, realising what Jesus was about to do, said: *"You shall never wash my feet!"* Jesus replied: *"If I do not wash you, you have no part with Me"* (John 13:8).

The purpose of the laver was thus explained by Jesus; those who wish to serve Him must be clean. When Jesus instructed His disciples to prepare a room for Him to observe Passover, Jesus said to them: *"A man will meet you carrying a pitcher of water; follow him into the house which he enters"* (Luke 22:10). Have you ever considered what the water was to be used for? Could it have been the water Jesus used to fill a basin (a type of laver), for Him to wash the feet of His disciples? The man with the water may not have been a co-incidence.

The laver was the only major item in the tabernacle for which no measurements are given – but its function is explained. Before entering the tent of meeting, the priests were told to wash their hands and feet. What took place at the laver, and was repeated by Jesus in the upper room as a lesson for His disciples, is what we are meant to do if we want to serve Jesus. Jesus said to His disciples: *"If I then, your Lord and Teacher, have washed your feet, you also ought to wash one another's feet. For I have given you an example, that you should do as I have done to you"* (John 13:14). Cleansing, symbolised by washing with water (water speaks to us of holiness), is our responsibility. James wrote: *'Pure and undefiled religion before God and the Father is this: to visit orphans and widows in their trouble and to keep oneself unspotted from the world'* (James 1:27). Jesus is willing and able to cleanse us from our sin, but the responsibility for maintaining a holy and godly life – and of serving others – is for us to carry out.

(6) **The Tent of Meeting** was erected by Moses on the first day of the first month. *'Then the LORD spoke to Moses, saying: "On the first day of the first month you shall set up the tabernacle of the tent of meeting. You shall put in it the ark of the Testimony, and partition off the ark with the veil"'* (Exodus 40:2–3). Was this timing so critical, for on the first day, of the first month, of the first year, God had said: *"Let there be light"* (Genesis 1:3)? As we shall see in study nine, this declaration by God is a clear reference to the Lord Jesus.

The materials used in the outer court were inferior to those used in the tent of meeting. What was so striking about the items placed in the tent of meeting was that they were either made of pure gold, or overlaid with pure gold. Gold was never used in the outer court. The church at Laodicea was told to: *"buy from Me gold refined in the fire, that you may be rich; and white garments* [righteousness]*, that you may be clothed"* (Revelation 3:18).

(7) **The Holy Place** – the larger of two rooms – was the place where the priests carried out their regular duties. The holy place measured ten cubits wide by twenty cubits long (4.6 x 9.2 meters); the measurements being a

combination of divine perfection and expectancy. What is remarkable is that despite the tabernacle's design, most of Israel's religious leaders failed to see Jesus as their Messiah. When Jerusalem's leaders rejected Jesus, the words of the prophet Isaiah, although perhaps not intended for this occasion, would have been entirely correct: *'For Jerusalem stumbled, and Judah is fallen, because their tongue and their doings are against the Lord, to provoke the eyes of His glory'* (Isaiah 3:8).

On one occasion when Jesus was visiting a home, not everyone was able to gain access, and so part of the roof had to be removed to enable a sick man to be lowered down to meet Jesus. During the time Jesus was there, the house became a holy place. Our holy place is where and when we spend time with Jesus.

(8) **The Golden Lampstand** – made of seven golden branches – provided light for the interior of the holy place. There were no windows in the holy place and so the lampstand was used to enable the priests to see and to perform their duties.

When the wise men arrived in Bethlehem to see Jesus, it was because they had seen His star, and they followed the star, *'till it came and stood over where the young Child was'* (Matthew 2:9). The place where Jesus was born became a holy place, and by the light of a star, wise men travelled to see Jesus. The shepherds who also came by night to see Jesus, came because *'the glory of the Lord shone around them'*, and the angel said to them: *"For there was born to you this day in the city of David a Savior, who is Christ the Lord"* (Luke 2:9–11). Jesus is God's heavenly light (Revelation 21:23).

Although no measurements for the lampstand are provided, a talent of gold was used in its construction. According to one source, a talent of gold was equal to the weight of an average man. Jesus said: *"I am the Light of the world. He who follows Me shall not walk in darkness but have the light of life"* (John 8:12).

(9) **The Table of Showbread** was made from acacia wood and overlaid with gold. Acacia wood speaks of the humanity of Jesus, the Son of Man; the gold speaks of His deity, the Son of God. On the table of showbread were placed twelve loaves (representative of the twelve tribes of Israel) and frankincense was then spread on the loaves for them to become a memorial offering to God. Frankincense was also one of the gifts the wise men brought to Jesus, representing His priestly appointment. The table of showbread was also an appointed place of communion, and today we recall the sacrifice of Jesus – the *'Bread of Life'* – at the communion table.

(10) **The Incense Altar** was the third item in the holy place, and was placed before the veil that divided the holy place from the holy-of-holies. The two materials used for the incense altar again portray the humanity and deity of Jesus – acacia wood overlaid with gold.

Each morning and each evening Aaron burnt incense at the incense altar, that its fragrance might fill the tent of meeting. Burning incense speaks of intercession, and Jesus is recorded as having spent time in prayer both in the mornings and in the evenings.

The purpose for the incense altar and the brazen altar are quite different. At the brazen altar (the cross), our sin is dealt with. At the incense altar, as we draw near to the holy-of-holies, we see the importance of prayer; for prayer enables us to enter God's presence.

The Greatest Thing in all my Life

Having observed Jesus portrayed in the holy place, we turn next to enter the holy-of-holies – the smaller of the two rooms. Before we do, I would like to refer to a worship song which was popular in the early 1970s.

1. The first line of the first verse: *'The greatest thing in all my life is knowing You.'*

2. The first line of the second verse: *'The greatest thing in all my life is loving You.'*

3. The first line of the third verse: *'The greatest thing in all my life is serving You.'*

In this song, the subsequent verse appears to contradict the previous verse – but this is not so. When we enter the outer court and observe the altar of burnt offering (the cross), we are introduced to Jesus; it is here we come to know Him. As we move into the holy place and observe the lampstand, the table of showbread, and the altar of incense, our relationship with Jesus changes, from knowing Him to loving Him. Finally, as we enter the holy-of-holies, how should we respond?

I thought of Isaiah who saw, *'The Lord sitting on a throne, high and lifted up and the train of His robe filled the temple. And one cried to another and said: "Holy, holy, holy is the Lord of hosts: the whole earth is full of His glory!"'* Isaiah then heard the Lord saying: *"Whom shall I send, and who will go for Us?"* to which Isaiah replied: *"Here am I, send me"* (Isaiah 6:1–8). Knowing Jesus and loving Jesus, comes before offering ourselves to Him in service. It is time to move through the veil.

(11) **The Veil** of the tabernacle divided the holy place from the holy-of-holies. The veil measured ten cubits by ten cubits (4.6 x 4.6 meters). Ten is the number of divine order. For Jesus, the event which confirmed His priestly appointment was the tearing in two of the temple veil, from top to bottom. With the introduction of the New Covenant, it established a new and living way for mankind to draw near to God.

'Therefore, brethren, having boldness to enter the Holiest by the blood of Jesus, by a new and living way which He consecrated for us through the <u>veil</u>, that is, <u>His flesh</u>, and having a high priest over the house of God, let us draw near with a true heart in full assurance

of faith, having our hearts sprinkled from an evil conscience and our bodies washed with pure water' (Hebrews 10:19–22).

As a result of Jesus' death, for those who wish to know and draw near to God, this is now possible. When one of the disciples asked Jesus to teach them how to pray, Jesus replied: *"When you pray, say: Our Father in heaven, hallowed be your name"* (Luke 11:1). For His disciples, the thought of ordinary people being able to pray directly to God would have been unusual – hence the question. Following the tearing of the temple veil, enabling access for all who wish to draw near to God, the sacrifice of Himself, a type of veil (Hebrews 10:20), is the (only) way that we can approach God.

(12) **The Holy-of-Holies** – the smaller of the two rooms – was where on the Day of Atonement the high priest presented the blood of the atonement sacrifice, which he sprinkled on the mercy seat of the Ark of the Covenant.

'But Christ came as high priest of the good things to come, with the greater and more perfect tabernacle not made with hands, that is, not of this creation. Not with the blood of goats and calves, but with His own blood, He entered The Most Holy Place once for all, having obtained eternal redemption' (Hebrews 9:11–12). *'For Christ has not entered the holy places made with hands, which are copies of the true, but into heaven itself, now to appear in the presence of God for us'* (9:24).

It is hard to imagine what it must have been like for Aaron to enter the holy-of-holies; however, from the books of Moses (Torah), Hebrews, and Revelation, we see that within the holy-of-holies was a three-fold (equal) manifestation of divine order. The holy-of-holies measured ten cubits, by ten cubits, by ten cubits (4.6 meters) – it was a cube. And the light in the holy-of-holies was not a natural light, or an artificial light, but was the light of the glory of God.

In the New Jerusalem, John saw: *'no temple in it, for the Lord God Almighty and the Lamb are its temple. The city had no need of the sun or the moon to shine in it, for the glory of God illuminated it. The Lamb is its Light'* (Revelation 21:2 & 22–23). But also, as with the holy-of-holies in the tabernacle, the City is a cube (Revelation 21:16). Thus was Israel's holy-of-holies; for it was a copy/image of greater things above.

To complete this study, because the last five items are closely related (in study three I provided a more detailed description of these five items); here I have provided only a brief recap.

(13) **The Ark of the Covenant** was made from acacia wood and overlaid with gold (and was likely to have resembled the manger in which Mary placed her new-born Son, the Lord Jesus).

(14) **The Mercy Seat** was the covering lid of the Ark of the Covenant and included two cherubim whose wings

touched (typifying the angels at Bethlehem when Jesus was born). The mercy seat represented the throne of God in the midst of His people.

The book of Hebrews informs us that within the Ark of the Covenant were placed three items.

(15) **The Golden Pot of Manna** which reminded Israel of God's provision for them.

(16) **Aaron's Rod** which signified God's authority.

(17) **The Ten Commandments** which were a reminder of how God's people were to conduct their lives.

The Ark of the Covenant

Whenever and wherever the Children of Israel travelled, they were told to follow the Ark of the Covenant. The day before they entered the Promised Land, Joshua said: *"Sanctify yourselves, for tomorrow the Lord will do wonders among you"* (Joshua 3:5). Sanctify means: *'To be Set Apart'*, and this is what the Children of Israel were told to do before they crossed the Jordan.

In referring to whenever the Children of Israel followed the Ark of the Covenant, so we are instructed to follow the Lord Jesus; that we might enter God's kingdom. The Ark of the Covenant was an archetype (as was Joseph) of the Lord Jesus. Before He began His public ministry, Jesus spent forty days in the wilderness prior to inaugurating the new and life giving way. His own forty days' experience corresponded numerically with the four hundred years the Children of Israel served the Egyptians as slaves, and the forty years they wandered in the wilderness before entering the Promised Land.

The Mercy Seat speaks of God's mercy and is in line with what we read in Psalm 23:6, *'Surely goodness and mercy shall follow me.'* God's mercy is His kindness. When King Solomon dedicated the first temple, *'The trumpeters and singers were as one, to make one sound to be heard in praising and thanking the LORD, and when they lifted up their voice with the trumpets and cymbals and instruments of music, and praised the LORD, saying: "For He is good, for His mercy endures forever"'* (2 Chronicles 5:13).

The Golden Pot of Manna assures God's people of His provision, for to trust God leads to hope. *'Now hope does not disappoint, because the love of God has been poured out in our hearts by the Holy Spirit who was given to us'* (Romans 5:5).

Aaron's Rod recalls the need to show respect for God's authority, knowing that: *'God resists the proud, but gives grace to the humble'* (James 4:6).

The Ten Commandments are God's modus operandi to show us the way of obedience, holiness, and peace with God, for to obey God is, *'for our profit, that we may be partakers of His holiness – without which no one will see the Lord'* (Hebrews 12:10 & 14).

Trust, respect and obedience are attributes that may not be so popular today as they once were; but they are not to be discounted as having less relevance today than in previous generations.

The tabernacle, which included all of its contents, points so clearly to the Lord Jesus, and explains a few of the foundations that Jews and Christians can observe and benefit from through studying their Hebrew Scriptures.

It is how Jesus demonstrated His love for Peter when He met with him on the shore of the Sea of Tiberias. Peter, plus six of the other disciples (John 21:2), who had fished all night without success, obeyed Jesus when He told them to let down their net on the other side of the boat. Their large catch of fish – described by John as a multitude of fish – confirmed Jesus' love for Peter and why Peter needed to know that Jesus had the authority to forgive and erase his three denials.

The cumulative total of adding one to two, two to three, and continuing up to seventeen (in the Hebrew idiom this sequence is known as: *'A Graduated Numerical Saying'* and in this example the numbers add up to one-hundred-and-fifty-three, the number of fish included in Peter's net), can assist us in our understanding of Jesus as the fulfillment of the tabernacle (which consisted of the seventeen major items as described in this study), and what the tabernacle was meant to represent: The presence of God in the midst of His people.

Whenever we consider Israel's tabernacle, or temple, it is right that we to think also of Jesus, and our need to worship Him. Therefore, if we add spiritual perfection to the perfection of divine order (7 + 10), the result is: *'The Perfection of Spiritual and Divine Order'*, and is an accurate assessment of who Jesus is – the Son of God who became the Son of Man.

Seven – Spiritual Perfection

From when Mary gave birth to Jesus in Bethlehem, to the commencement of His public ministry, Jesus was revealed to individuals, or groups of different people, on seven specific occasions.

1. At the time of His birth, for Joseph and Mary, Jesus was revealed as the *'Son of God'*.

2. For the shepherds who visited Jesus at the manger in Bethlehem, Jesus was revealed as the *'Good Shepherd'*.

3. To the wise men who came to worship Jesus because they had seen His star, Jesus was revealed as the *'King of Kings'*.

4. To Simeon, a serving priest, Jesus was revealed as the *'High Priest'* of God.

5. To Anna, a prophetess from the tribe of Asher, Jesus was revealed as the *'Prophet of God'*.

6. At the age of twelve, when Jesus was found by Joseph and Mary sitting in the midst of teachers, Jesus was revealed as the *'Teacher'*.

7. Finally, for John the Baptist, Jesus was revealed as: *"Behold! The Lamb of God who takes away the sin of the world!"* (John 1:29).

Ten – the Perfection of Divine Order

In the book of Hebrews there is a ten-fold description of our relationship with God. It describes the progression from the Old Covenant to the New Covenant, and is why when Jesus made His final visit to Jerusalem, many of the religious Jews were not prepared to alter their beliefs or change their status quo; for the fact Jesus spoke of a new way, a better way, was seen as being a challenge to their traditional way of doing religion.

Therefore, for those who believe in Jesus…

1. *But you have come to Mount Zion,*

2. *And to the city of the living God,*

3. *The heavenly Jerusalem,*

4. *To an innumerable company of angels,*

5. *To the general assembly and church of the firstborn,*

6. *Who are registered in heaven,*

7. *To God the judge of all,*

8. *To the spirits of just men made perfect,*

9. *To Jesus the Mediator of the new covenant,*

10. *And to the blood of sprinkling that speaks better things than that of Abel.* (Hebrews 12:22–24).

Historically, the original for the perfection of spiritual and divine order was Israel's tabernacle in which seventeen (main) objects and/or locations are given. When seen individually, each of these objects/locations can assist us in our understanding of Jesus and how He fulfills the reason why God instructed Moses to make a tabernacle.

At the commencement of this study, I said concerning the tabernacle, it was the most important man-made object in the whole of human creation – because of who it represented. In the process, I have also referred to the way numbers appear in Scripture, explaining briefly the importance and relevance of numbers.

A further aspect is how God ordered Moses to position the camps of the tribes of Israel around the tabernacle. In Numbers chapter two (is it not intriguing that the fourth book in the Bible is called *'Numbers'*?) we find listed the numbers of each of the twelve tribes of Israel and how their families were to be camped on the four sides of the tabernacle (which is not a minor detail).

On the east side (the side where the entrance gate into the tabernacle was positioned), the tribes of Judah, Issachar and Zebulun were camped. On the west side, the tribes of Ephraim, Manasseh, and Benjamin. On the north side, the tribes of Dan, Asher, and Naphtali. On the south side, the tribes of Reuben, Simeon, and Gad.

Numbers chapter two also lists the numbers of the twelve tribes. On the east side, the numbers represented 31% of the people; the west side 18% of the people; the south side 25% of the people; the north side 26% of the people. When viewed from above – and with the east side at the bottom – a drone view of the camp may have represented a cross, such as the cross on which Jesus died. And in the heart of the camp was the tabernacle of meeting where God visited and dwelt with His people, which, as we have seen in numerous ways, represented the Lord Jesus (see diagram on page 112).

From when Jesus died (then He rose from the dead), Israel's imperfect way of approaching God came to an end – because Jesus is the supreme way. I believe this is why Israel's temple in Jerusalem, which was destroyed by the Romans in 70 C.E., has never been rebuilt. To have continued with the practice of sacrificing animals as a means of seeking God's forgiveness – when Jesus has paid the full price for sin – would have been an affront to God; for God gave to us His Son.

****

Camped on the
WEST SIDE
were the tribes of
Ephraim,
Manasseh, and
Benjamin.
18%

Camped on the
SOUTH SIDE
were the tribes of
Reuben, Simeon, and
Gad. 25%

Camped on the
NORTH SIDE
were the tribes of Dan,
Asher, and Naphtali.
26%

The Tabernacle

Camped on the
EAST SIDE were
the tribes of Judah,
Issachar, and
Zebulun.
31%

Shown on the previous page, a diagrammatic view of how the families of Israel were camped around the tabernacle. The percentages refer to the collective number of people as they were positioned on each of the four sides of the tabernacle. The Levites, the priestly tribe, were camped on the four sides in the immediate area surrounding the tabernacle. (See Numbers 1–3). Notice how the layout – determined by numbers – could have resembled a cross. Also note how the bottom of the cross would have been on the eastern side, the side where the entrance of the tabernacle would have been. Thus the layout of the camp of the Children of Israel, which included the tabernacle, would have depicted the cross on which Jesus died as it would have appeared to those who watched when Jesus was crucified.

On the next four pages there are fifteen questions which are based on this study. The suggested answers can be found on pages 220–221.

Study 4 Questions — The Tabernacle

1. What was the tabernacle Moses was told to make for the Children of Israel used for?

ANSWER: _____

2. What did the curtain, which was made of fine white linen and formed the outer perimeter of the outer court of the tabernacle, represent?

ANSWER: _____

3. Why was it said that the shedding of innocent blood is the only way sin can be removed? (Leviticus 17:11 & Hebrews 9:22).

ANSWER: _____

---

4. Within the outer court was a bronze laver, a container of water used by the priests to wash their hands and feet before they performed their priestly duties (Exodus 30:17–21). When and how did Jesus use a laver in order to set an example for His disciples? (John 13:1–5).

ANSWER: _____

---

5. The tent of meeting, positioned towards the western end of the outer court, was like a large tent and was divided into two rooms. Name the two rooms the tent of meeting was divided into. (Exodus 26:31–33).

ANSWER: _____

6. The larger of the two rooms had no windows, and so a golden lampstand was used to provide artificial light. The golden lampstand had a number of branches, or lights, in which purified oil was used as fuel. How many lights, or branches, did the golden lampstand have? (Exodus 25:31–40).

ANSWER: _____

7. Two other items were placed in the larger of the two rooms. Give the names of these two items. (Exodus 40:22–27).

ANSWER: _____

8. A curtain was used to divide the two rooms of the tent of meeting. What was this curtain called? (Exodus 40:21). Two words.

ANSWER: _____

9. When Jesus was being crucified and the sun was darkened, what happened to this curtain and why do you think it happened? (Luke 23:44–45). You may like to refer to Hebrews 10:19–22.

ANSWER: _____

_____

_____

10. There were no windows or artificial light within the smaller of the two rooms. How was this room illuminated? (Exodus 40:34). See also Revelation 22:5.

ANSWER: _____

_____

11. What was the piece of furniture called that was placed within the second, or inner, room?

ANSWER: _____

12. Israel's high priest entered the smaller of the two rooms on only one day a year. Which day in the Hebrew calendar – one of Israel's annual times of remembrance – did the high priest enter this room? (Leviticus 16).

ANSWER: _____

13. How did Jesus eclipse what had been central to Israel's way of approaching God? (Hebrews 9:11–12 & 24–26).

ANSWER: _____

_____

14. Solomon's temple, which was built to replace the tabernacle, then re-built by Nehemiah after the seventy years of captivity in Babylon, and again re-built by Herod the Great, was destroyed by the Romans in 70 C.E. Why do you think Israel's temple has never been rebuilt?

ANSWER: _____

_____

15. According to Revelation 21, there is to be: *'A new heaven, a new earth, and a new Jerusalem, coming down out of heaven from God'*. In Isaiah 66:1, we read: *"Heaven is My throne and earth is My footstool. Where is the house that you will build Me? And where is the place of My rest?"* Where did Solomon place the Ark of the Covenant and what did God say of this place regarding His name? (I Kings 8:6 & 29).

ANSWER: _____

_____

INTRODUCTION TO STUDIES FIVE–NINE

For the remaining five studies, I will be referring to a number of Old and New Testament scriptures which appear to indicate a particular day for the birth of Jesus. Whilst the death of Jesus paved the way for the introduction of the Christian gospel (for without His death there would be no *'Pass-Over'*, no forgiveness), generally speaking, Jesus' birth has been moderated by the adoption of Christmas as the time when Jesus was born. Many agree however, that today's celebration of the birth of Jesus has become indeterminate from what His birth really means; so is there a more appropriate day, a biblical day, that points to when Jesus was born?

In a previous book, I wrote about signs in the Bible for when Jesus was most likely to have been born. When I sent the draft of the manuscript to Dr. Tony Stone, a British-born Jew who is a trustee serving on the board of Christ for all Nations UK, Dr. Stone kindly replied to my request to write the Foreword. At this juncture, I have included Dr. Stone's comments on my research, for I feel they may assist the reader as an introduction to the five remaining studies. Dr. Stone's reply included…

These studies explore a question that has challenged the church for centuries and challenges traditional thinking and adds a biblical dimension, well thought through and scripturally supported throughout. If read with an open mind, [they] can only bring the reader to the point of making a decision relating to a very important subject. The argument is convincing, well presented and will undoubtedly cause a re-thinking for many.

In addition to the main subject, I was greatly blessed by the five points used to present the writer's conviction. Each is a complete study in itself. To have a copy of [these studies] *is to gain a five-book library of good, solid, biblical teaching. Any one of the five is a book in itself, and I found myself wonderfully enlightened on great truths of the word of God.*

Whilst each reader will be challenged to a personal conviction to the conclusions of this excellent piece of work and research, I am convinced that [these studies] *should be read widely as a source of biblical information that is nothing short of 'A Treasury of Teaching'. I would particularly recommend them to anyone who has a thirst for learning more of God.*

Dr. Tony Stone

I wish to thank Dr. Stone for his kind endorsement of studies five to nine.

STUDY 5 – WHEN WAS JESUS REALLY BORN?

'And it came to pass that a decree went out from Caesar Augustus that all the world should be registered. So Joseph went up from Galilee, out of the city of Nazareth, to Bethlehem, to be registered with Mary, his betrothed wife, who was with child. So it was, while they were there, she brought forth her firstborn Son, and wrapped Him in swaddling cloths, and laid Him in a manger, because there was no room for them in the inn' (Luke 2:1–7).

On Friday, July 1, 2011, Jonathan Sacks, who at the time was the Chief Rabbi of Great Britain, said on BBC Radio Four's *'Thought for the Day'* programme...

"In one sense life is a lottery, because none of us chooses when and where to be born."

How true, not one of us had any say in the matter; but there has been one exception, for only Jesus (together with His Father) knew when and where He would be born. Shortly before Jesus was led away to be crucified, and while He was still with His disciples, Jesus prayed to His Father: *"And now, O Father, glorify Me together with yourself, with the glory I had with You <u>before</u> the world was ... for You loved Me <u>before</u> the foundation of the world"* ((John 17:5 & 24).

The birth of Jesus was a planned event and it was Micah the prophet who prophesied where the birth of Jesus was to take place. *'But you, Bethlehem Ephrathah, though you are little among the thousands of Judah, yet out of you shall come forth to Me the One to be Ruler in Israel, whose goings forth are from of old, from everlasting'* (Micah 5:2). And the writer of Psalm two refers to the day when Jesus was to be born: *'You are My Son, today I have begotten You'* (Psalm 2:7).

Therefore, from these two scriptures, it appears God did indeed select Bethlehem as the place for His Son's birth, and a certain day for when His birth was to take place. The question which all believers might ask themselves is this: *"Which day is the psalmist referring to?"*

Was Jesus Born at Christmas?

It was in 2010 that I first began to consider when it was that Jesus was born, and if the date had been recorded. Because many assume the day of Jesus' birth was not recorded, it is then permissible to remember His birth at Christmas. In a similar way, although the death of Jesus took place at the time of the Jewish festival of Passover, most people remember His death at Easter – but what if there is no biblical hypothesis for either assumption?

Lunar and Solar Cycles

What I first began to study was the link that connects the lunar calendar that Jewish people observe, with the solar calendar that Gentiles follow. It is clear Jesus kept the lunar calendar, but His life in terms of years would have followed the solar calendar. That the time of His birth and His death can be traced to both calendars is quite remarkable, yet it also makes perfect sense.

We know that Jesus was (jointly) involved in creation, *'through whom also He made the worlds'* (Hebrews 1:2), and so his birth-day could not have been a random event. The time (or day) of Jesus' birth was when He became: *'Immanuel ... God with us'* (Matthew 1:23).

The New Testament teaches that for those who believe in Jesus, they are to honour His death; so why would the Bible be silent when it comes to honoring His birth? Is the pattern we keep of remembering our own births, the births of our loved ones and our friends, far removed from God (and us) remembering Jesus' birth?

When Jesus died, the time was recorded. He died at the ninth hour on the 14th day of the Hebrew month Nisan, the eve of Passover (Mark 15:34). Knowing when Jesus died can be helpful in determining when He was born, for Luke wrote that when Jesus began His ministry, He was: *'about thirty years of age'* (Luke 3:23).

Joseph was also thirty years old when he began his life's calling (Genesis 41:46). Age thirty was also the time when the sons of Levi commenced serving in the tabernacle – referred to in the book of Numbers chapter four, no less than seven times.

Weeks and Years

In Hebrew thought, a week can be described as a period of seven days, seven weeks, or seven years. Daniel the prophet wrote: *'Messiah shall be cut off, but not for Himself'* – and when this would take place. *'But in the middle of the week He shall bring an end to sacrifice and offering'* (Daniel 9:26–27).

It is agreed by many scholars – including Eusebius, a Christian writer of the fourth century, who wrote: *'Now the whole period of our Saviour's teaching and working of miracles is said to have been three-and-a-half years, which is half a week'* – that we can conclude from this prophecy in Daniel, the ministry of Jesus was designed to last for three-and-a-half years before He would be cut off and die. This same expression of being *'cut off'* was also used by Isaiah. *'For He was cut off from the land of the living'* (Isaiah 53:8). When Jesus died, He would have been thirty-three-and-a-half years of age.

Hebrew years are based on the lunar calendar and are linked to the moon's circumnavigation of the earth; but lunar years lag behind solar years because solar years are measured by the earth's movement around the sun; and so solar years are longer, by about eleven days. About every three years, an extra month is added to the Hebrew lunar calendar to bring its cycle into line with the solar cycle. This is carried out so that lunar years do not get out of phase with the earth's seasons.

It was in 2010 that I carried out a simple calculation. By referring to 2009 and 2010 lunar cycles, I superimposed the two lunar cycles over a solar year for each of the two years, and then worked backwards from the 14th day of Nisan (in 2010, this was Monday, March 29th), the day in the lunar calendar when Jesus died, half a solar year.

The calculation (although it may appear complex) was quite straightforward. However, it was the outcome that took me by surprise. It took me to the Hebrew Day of Atonement in the previous year, the tenth day of Tishrei (in 2009, this was Monday, September 28th).

Previously, I had no idea there could be a lunar and solar connection between the Day of Atonement in one year, and the day before Passover in the following year, the day when Jesus died. However, the two dates, exactly half a solar year apart (180 degrees of a solar cycle), appeared to indicate a day (and a time) for when Jesus was born.

At His birth, the destiny of Jesus was for Him to fulfil what God had said should take place in the tabernacle's holy-of-holies on the Day of Atonement. That is, for the high priest to enter God's presence on behalf of God's people. When Jesus died on the eve of Passover (180 degrees of a solar cycle), He would then fulfill and become God's Passover sacrifice (1 Corinthians 5:7).

The dates for the Day of Atonement and for Passover were not selected lightly; they were chosen by God who then informed Moses of His decision. The writer Abraham Joshua Heschel (1907–1972), provides the key reason for this: *'God is not in things of space, but in moments of time. Yet the likeness of God can be found in time, which is eternity in disguise. The Bible is more concerned with time than with space. It sees the world in the dimension of time.'*

On a number of occasions, Jesus said His hour (His time) had not yet come; for example, when He turned water into wine, or when some tried to kill Him. Only when His time on earth had come to an end did God permit Jesus to die, so that His birth and His death might become the fulfillment for the Day of Atonement and the Passover times of remembrance.

The synoptic gospels (Matthew, Mark, and Luke) each record that Jesus died at the ninth hour (three o'clock in the afternoon) on the 14th day of Nisan. If the birth of Jesus occurred at precisely one hundred and eighty degrees into the solar cycle from when He died – which is half a solar year, or one hundred and eighty-two days, fourteen hours, fifty-four minutes and thirty seconds as calculated in reverse from the time of His death – then Jesus could have been born at five-and-a-half minutes after midnight on the Day of Atonement, thirty-three-and-a-half solar years earlier.

Although I cannot prove this was when Jesus was born (it would be presumptuous to say so), the *fact* it can be exactly half a solar year from the Day of Atonement in one year, to the eve of preparing for the Passover in the following year, for myself is very compelling. Did God indeed plan for the birth of His Son to be linked to earth's journey around the sun; for Scripture (and also science) confirms that the sun, moon and the earth's rotation on its axis, control the length of our days, the four seasons, and earth's repeating cycle of time.

The Bible states that the heavens are God's masterpiece. Psalm 19:1 – *'The heavens declare the glory of God; and the firmament shows His handiwork'*. Therefore, is it so surprising there may be a connection between the establishment of these three celestial bodies, and the time of Jesus' birth? Because, *'God in these last days has spoken to us by His Son ... through whom also He made the worlds'* (Hebrews 1:1–2), could not the time for Jesus' birth be traced to the heavenlies, long before – and seemingly after – Jesus was born?

At His first coming, Jesus fulfilled many of the Bible's prophetic signs – such as the Hebrew festivals. At His second coming, He will fulfill further prophetic signs, some of which He shared with His disciples and which will include: *"Signs in the sun, in the moon, and in the stars; and on the earth distress of nations, with perplexity, the sea and the waves roaring; men's hearts failing them from fear and the expectation of those things which are coming on the earth, for the powers of the heavens will be shaken"* (Luke 21:25–26).

Two New Years

Hebrew lunar years feature two new years. The Jewish people's civil calendar begins in the autumn with the month Tishrei. If Jesus was born on the tenth day of Tishrei, the Day of Atonement, it was appropriate, for His birth was a civil event. Their religious calendar begins in the spring with the month Nisan. Jesus died on the fourteenth day of Nisan; the eve of Passover, for His death was a religious event.

Most are aware that a solar year lasts for three hundred and sixty-five days, and that during every fourth year an extra day is added to keep our years in step with the earth's orbit around the sun. To satisfy my curiosity as to the actual time it takes for us to travel millions of miles through space, I turned to the internet. The time taken for the earth to circumnavigate the sun is three hundred and sixty-five days, five hours and forty-nine minutes (plus a few seconds). It was this length of time which I divided by two that led me to discover it can be exactly half a solar year from the Day of Atonement in one year, to the eve of Passover in the following year.

What is also riveting is we are traveling through space at a speed of approximately 66,600 miles-per-hour, and in each year in our journey around the sun, we will have travelled 584 million miles. And in our journey through both time and space, it is to a programmed accuracy of less than one second a year! Included in this blend of time, space and physical movement is the moon, which orbits the earth once every twenty-nine-and-a-half days. The moon's orbit of the earth explains why Hebrew lunar months and years are shorter than the earth's solar years – by about eleven days.

The earth is also tilted from the perpendicular and it is this angle that determines the earth's seasons, which in turn controls the earth's weather and our ability to survive; mainly through the seasonal harvests.

The earth's tilt from the perpendicular by twenty-three degrees (technologists say it is the most suitable angle) is a number (23) we will return to in the next study.

The forces which control the movement of the earth and the moon around the sun control life's sustainability. Creation equals design, and the sun, moon and the earth are a prime example of a perfect triune relationship; for God made the three to function as one. To see Jesus as He, *'through whom also He made the worlds'*, is to see that God has established a plan, and His plan is one that includes the union He has with His Son and the Holy Spirit, and the relationship He has with His people.

The likelihood of Jesus' birth being associated with the establishment of creation and the yearly cycle of the seven Hebrew (biblical) festivals, which includes the Day of Atonement, suggests the day of Jesus' birth is not so incomprehensible as some may have imagined, but that the day of His birth can be seen as a help to faith, to believe in God, a sign that God was in Christ reconciling the world to Himself and not imputing (attributing) our sins to ourselves (2 Corinthians 5:19).

In choosing the day for the Day of Atonement, Leviticus 16:1–2 stresses its importance. *'Now the LORD spoke to Moses after the death of the two sons of Aaron, when they offered profane fire before the LORD, and died'* (Verse 1). For Aaron, it must have been the worst day of his life. To lose a son is sad, but to lose two sons and on the same day; for Aaron it was a personal tragedy.

When setting aside the Day of Atonement (the day Aaron was told to enter the holy-of-holies on behalf of the people as their representative), the Lord then said to Moses: *"Tell Aaron your brother not to come at just any time into the Holy Place inside the veil, before the mercy seat which is on the ark, lest he die; for I will appear in the cloud above the mercy seat"* (verse 2).

There is an emphasis here on: *'At just any time'*, and recalls the time when God Himself appeared in the cloud above the mercy seat, and that He elected to do so on the Hebrew Day of Atonement. God, surely, must have had a very good reason for choosing this day for His appearance above the mercy seat? Could it be the Day of Atonement is to be recognized as a token of God's commitment (via His Son) to His people as seen in the ceremony that is still kept by Jewish people (and a few Gentiles) to the present day?

Worship the Son, not the Sun

Although in this study I have highlighted the importance of the sun and the moon in controlling our days, years, and the seasons (and the time when Jesus was born), this is not to say we should regard the sun or the moon as aids in our worship. In the early days of Josiah's reign, idolatrous priests, *'burned incense to Baal, to the sun, to the moon, to the constellations and to all the host of heaven'* (2 Kings 23:5). Clearly this was wrong, and Josiah took the necessary steps to remove from Israel these pagan rituals.

The Bible teaches we are not to regard the constellations as anything other than physical/created entities. When it comes to our worship, Jesus taught: *"God is Spirit, and those who worship Him must worship in spirit and truth"* (John 4:23). In Revelation we are told: *"Fear God and give glory to Him ... and worship Him who made heaven and earth, the sea and springs of water"* (Revelation 14:7). God has designed us to honour and worship our maker, not created or man-made things. And it is God who sent Jesus, who: *'When He had by Himself purged our sins, sat down at the right hand of the Majesty on high'* (Hebrews 1:3; see also Romans 8:34). The hallmark of the Christian faith (derived from its Hebrew foundations), is that we worship God and His Son – not the sun, moon or the constellations.

****

When was Jesus Really Born?

Chart showing how in 2009/2010, the time from the Day of Atonement to Passover was precisely half a year.

This chart looks forwards from the Day of Atonement in 2009, the tenth day of Tishri, to the eve of Passover in 2010, the 14th day of Nisan. (In some years the Hebrew months Heshvan and Kislev may have 29 days, or 30 days, depending on the lunar cycle).

11th to 30th Tishri:	20:00 days
1st to 30th Heshvan:	30:00 days
1st to 30th Kislev:	30:00 days
1st to 29th Tevet:	29:00 days
1st to 30th Shevat:	30:00 days
1st to 29th Adar:	29:00 days
1st to 13th Nisan:	13:00 days
Total number of complete days:	181.00 days

Add 23:00 hours, 54.5 minutes. The 10th day of Tishri. (The Day of Atonement, from 00:05.5 hours). *

Add 15 hours. The 14th day of Nisan to 3:00 p.m. (When Jesus died at the eve of Passover). **

* Add 23 hours, 54.5 minutes.
**Add 15 hours. Total: 38 hours, 54.5 minutes.

This equals 1 day (plus 14 hours, 54.5 minutes).	1:00 day
Total number of complete days:	182.00 days

Add 14 hours, 54.5 minutes. = 182 days, 14 hours, 54.5 minutes. This is exactly half of a Solar year; a Solar year being 365 days, 5 hours and 49 minutes (plus a few seconds).

FOOTNOTE

In Luke 3:23, we read: *'Now Jesus Himself began His ministry at about thirty years of age'*. I have been asked the following question: *"Does this mean Jesus was not precisely thirty years old when He began His ministry."*

A person's life is measured by the number of solar years they have lived, not lunar years, for lunar years are shorter than solar years as explained in this study. When Jesus began His ministry, it would have been difficult to ascertain precisely how old He was, for lunar years are linked to the keeping of the Hebrew (Jewish) festivals.

But also, we know from John's Gospel, that before He began His ministry, Jesus and His mother Mary were invited to a wedding, and it was here that His mother informed Jesus that the master of the wedding had run out of wine. Jesus said to His mother: *"Woman, what does your concern have to do with Me? My hour has not yet come"* (John 2:4). Which was the *hour* Jesus was referring to? Was He aware He was still in His late twenties? When reading the Bible, what we must not do is to ignore its minor details. Mary's response was to say to the servants: *"Whatever He says to you, do it."* (John 2:5). Mary knew her Son was not too rigid.

For many years there has been confusion about the dates we should observe when remembering the birth and death of Jesus. Much of this confusion has arisen because of the changes made to the solar calendar – for example, most continue to remember the death of Jesus on Good Friday, and His resurrection on Easter Sunday – but that is not three days and three nights.

Regarding the time observed for Easter, Wikipedia explains: *'The Gregorian calendar* [solar years] *is the most widely used calendar. Named after Pope Gregory XIII who introduced it in October 1582, it is a refinement of the Julian calendar amounting to a 0.002% correction in the length of the year. The motivation for the reform was to bring the date for Easter to the time of year in which it was celebrated when it was introduced by the early church. Because Easter was tied to the spring equinox, the Roman Catholic Church considered the steady drift in the date of Easter, caused by the year being slightly too long, to be undesirable. The Gregorian reform was adopted by most countries for the sake of convenience in international trade.'*

So there we have it; not an ideal situation, nevertheless, an explanation that is based on Church (Gentile) history, rather than what the Hebrew Bible teaches us.

On the next two pages there are seven questions which are based on this study. The suggested answers can be found on page 222.

Study 5 Questions – When was Jesus Born?

1. Jesus prayed: *"Father ... You loved Me before the foundation of the world"* (John 17:24). What does this say to us about who Jesus is and when His life began?

ANSWER: _____

_____

_____

2. What was the name of the prophet who wrote Bethlehem was to be the birth-place of Jesus? (See Matthew 2:5–6).

ANSWER: _____

3. Jesus was (*'about'* – Luke 3:23) thirty years old when He began His ministry. In Numbers chapter four, how many times does it state the Levites had to be thirty years of age before they could serve in the tabernacle?

ANSWER: _____

4. How long was the ministry of Jesus designed to last for? (Daniel 9:26–27).

ANSWER: _____

5. On which day in the Hebrew calendar did Jesus die? The Bible describes it as on the eve of one of Israel's annual seven times of remembrance. In Matthew 27:62, it describes it as being *'The Day of Preparation'*.

ANSWER: _____

_____

6. Who decided when Israel was to keep the seven Hebrew festivals – known by Jews as the seven times of remembrance? (Leviticus 23).

ANSWER: _____

7. List Israel's seven annual festivals. Details can be found in Leviticus 23. Note: In this chapter, the importance of the Sabbath is given first. Do not include the Sabbath in your answer.

ANSWER: _____

_____

_____

_____

_____

****

STUDY 6 – PSALM 23

Having observed a lunar/solar link to the birth-day of Jesus, I still felt I needed to see additional evidence in Scripture to confirm my initial discovery. A short time after I had observed the lunar/solar sign, as I left our home to take our dog for a walk, I asked the Lord if the timing for the birth of Jesus was again recorded in Scripture. As I prayed, I felt an urge to consider one of David's Psalms. Following my walk with Suzie, and as I read through the Psalm, I saw that a thousand years before Jesus was born, David appears to have been provided with detailed information about the timing of Jesus' birth; plus six other features of His unique life.

The Psalm I turned to was Psalm 23, and in reading through this much-loved Psalm, I saw seven portraits, each of which corresponds to the seven festivals of the Lord as described in Leviticus chapter 23.

Psalm 23 and Passover – Part One
(Leviticus 23:4–5).

'The LORD is my Shepherd; I shall not want. He makes me to lie down in green pastures; He leads me beside the still waters.'

The first four stanzas of Psalm 23 are associated with God's provision of a Passover lamb – the Lord Jesus. When Jesus entered Jerusalem on a young donkey, the date was the tenth day of the Hebrew month Nisan. It was the same day of the same month the priests would have made a selection of a lamb without blemish for Passover (Exodus 12:3–5). It was also the same day of the same month the Children of Israel had crossed the Jordan to enter the Promised Land (Joshua 4:19). Four days later, on the fourteenth of Nisan (Exodus 12:6), the Passover lamb was slain. It was the same day that Jesus died, and so the opening four stanzas of Psalm 23 lead us to recall Jesus as being God's chosen Passover Lamb.

When John the Baptist saw Jesus coming towards him, he said: *"Behold! The Lamb of God who takes away the sin of the world!"* (John 1:29). When we think of Jesus and how John the Baptist described Him, and then as we read the opening stanzas of Psalm 23, is it not the Lord Jesus we should be seeing as God's Passover Lamb?

'He restores my soul.'

When the time came for Jesus to die, He became very disturbed and said: *"Now My soul is troubled, and what shall I say? "Father, save Me from this hour"? But for this purpose I came to this hour. Father, glorify Your name."* Then a voice came from heaven, saying: *"I have both glorified it and will glorify it again"* (John 12:27–28).

When Jesus prayed to His Father, we are told His soul was troubled and was in need of comfort. It was then that His Father responded to encourage His Son, with an audible voice which was heard from heaven, in order to restore His Son's soul – *'He restores my soul'.*

Psalm 23 and the Feast of Unleavened Bread
(Leviticus 23:6–8).

When Passover and the first day of the Feast of Unleavened Bread were first instituted, they took place at the same time, from twilight on the 14th day of Nisan, through to the evening of the 15th day (Exodus 12:6 & 18). Luke identifies these two times of remembrance as being one. *'Now the Feast of Unleavened Bread drew near, which is called Passover'* (Luke 22:1). And the prophet Ezekiel also refers to these two times as being one: *'In the first month, on the fourteenth day of the month, you shall observe the Passover, a feast of seven days; unleavened bread shall be eaten'* (Ezekiel 45:21).

At Passover and the Feast of Unleavened Bread there is an overlap. Passover recalls how God freed His people from slavery in Egypt (as today we can be set-free from the slavery of our sin). Unleavened bread represents righteousness; that God's people might become holy, or righteous, because of our need to live a holy life.

When leaven is mentioned in the Bible, it often refers to sin, and Pilate, having examined Jesus in a similar way as the priests would have examined the Passover lamb for any defects before it was sacrificed, announced three times to those who were demanding His death: *'I find no fault in Him'* (John 18:38, 19:4 & 19:6). Because

Jesus was without fault, without sin, He fulfilled the keeping of the unleavened bread requirement, and in an identical way as it had been observed at the time of the Exodus of the Children of Israel from Egypt. Therefore, in the words of the 6th stanza in Psalm 23:3, we read:

'He leads me in the paths of righteousness for His name's sake.'

Psalm 23 and Passover – Part Two (Leviticus 23:4–5).

The next four stanzas of Psalm 23 return us to the theme of Passover, for they portray how Jesus – God's chosen Passover Lamb, the *'Lamb of God'* – suffered so that the consequences of sin, our sin, might be atoned for.

'Yea, though I walk through the valley of the shadow of death, I will fear no evil; for You are with me; Your rod and Your staff, they comfort me.'

In the Jewish Study Bible the first phrase is rendered as: *'Though I walk through a valley of deepest darkness.'* Not only does this darkness recall the time when Jesus was in Gethsemane in the Kidron Valley (in Hebrew the name of this valley means: *'The Valley where Yahweh shall judge'*), but also the darkness which took place as Jesus was dying. Jesus knew He was destined to suffer extreme pain and death, yet He had no need to fear the consequences of death (as many do), for He was sinless.

The words from Psalm 23:4, *'Your rod and Your staff'* (recalling Aaron's rod and Moses' staff), may refer to

God exercising His authority (His permissive will) being carried out in order to provide for our salvation.

Psalm 23 and the Feast of Firstfruits
(Leviticus 23:10–14).

The third of the seven Hebrew feasts – the Hebrew word for feast means: *'Appointed Times'* – is to celebrate the start of the barley harvest and this is why at the Feast of Firstfruits there is much rejoicing and sharing of food.

In the the 11th stanza of Psalm 23 we read:

'You prepare a table before me in the presence of my enemies.'

Prior to His valley of the shadow of death experience, Jesus was surrounded by His enemies; from religious leaders and false witnesses, to Roman soldiers who so cruelly mocked Him and then nailed Him to a cross. However, three days later, on the first day of the week, Jesus overcame their rejection as He rose from the dead.

Paul wrote: *'But now is Christ risen from the dead and has become the firstfruits of those who have fallen asleep'* (1Corinthians 15:20). The apostle's reference to *'firstfruits'*, points to Jesus' resurrection being linked to the Hebrew festival of Firstfruits, for this feast was observed on the first day of the week after the start of the barley harvest (Leviticus 23:10–14). It was the most appropriate day for Jesus to rise from the dead.

Psalm 23 and a Table

A table (Psalm 23:5), is an item of furniture that is referred to throughout the Bible. In nearly every place where the word *'Table'* occurs, it is usually associated with a meal. On the day of Jesus' resurrection, two of His disciples journeyed from Jerusalem to Emmaus, a distance of seven miles. *'So it was, while they conversed and reasoned* [with each other], *that Jesus Himself drew near and went with them'* (Luke 24:15). However, the two disciples failed to recognize Him, for: *'their eyes were restrained so that they did not know Him'* (Luke 24:16). When Jesus spoke to them, He began: *'At Moses and all the Prophets, He expounded to them in all the Scriptures the things concerning Himself'* (Luke 24:27).

As they drew near to the village where they were going, *'He* [Jesus] *indicated that He would have gone farther, but they constrained Him, saying, "Abide with us, for it is toward evening, and the day is far spent." And He went in to stay with them. Now it came to pass, as He sat at the <u>table</u> with them, that He took bread, blessed it and broke it, and gave it to them. Then their eyes were opened and they knew Him; and He vanished from their sight'* (Luke 24:28–31).

This passage recalls Psalm 23:5 – **'You prepare a table before me in the presence of my enemies'** – and describes what took place as the enemies of Jesus, who remained vigilant to the threat of His resurrection, placed guards at His tomb. Jesus, of course, was not constrained by guards; but He appeared to two of His disciples and shared a meal with them at a **_table_**, and He did so on the day of His resurrection and at the time of the Jewish festival of Firstfruits. Regarding persecution, Jewish people have a saying: *'They tried to kill us. We survived. Let's eat!'* Similar words may also be applied to Jesus: *"They tried to kill Me. I survived. Let's eat!"*

Psalm 23 and the Feast of Weeks (Leviticus 23:15–22).

Seven Sabbaths (seven weeks) and one day later (fifty days) and the Feast of Weeks is held to celebrate the wheat harvest. Today, Christians recall this feast as the time when: *'The Day of Pentecost had fully come'* (Acts 2:1) and the Holy Spirit was poured out on the disciples and those who had become followers of Jesus, and was witnessed by, *'tongues, as of fire, and one sat upon each of them'* (Acts 2:3).

In recalling the wheat harvest (Feast of Weeks), after the disciples had been filled with the Holy Spirit and following Peter's first sermon, about three thousand people were baptized and added to the Church (Acts 2:41). It was the first harvest of people and was in line with the biblical harvest of the Feast of Weeks.

Although the anointing of the disciples by the Holy Spirit took place at the time of the Feast of Weeks; at Bethany, *'A woman came to Him having an alabaster flask of very costly fragrant oil, and she poured it on His head as He sat at the table'* (Matthew 26:7). Therefore, for Jesus and His promise to His disciples, the 12th stanza in Psalm 23:5 recalls:

'You anoint my head with oil.'

Psalm 23 and the Garden of Gethsemane (Luke 22).

'My cup runs over.'

In the words of the next stanza, I have not been able to see a direct connection to the seven feasts of the Lord; nevertheless, its inclusion comes at the Psalm's pivotal point. Do not underestimate what Jesus must felt in the Garden of Gethsemane (its name means: *'Olive Press'*). Gethsemane is a reminder of the process involved in extracting oil from olives, when they are crushed four times to extract every last drop of oil. On the eve of Passover, being crushed in Gethsemane is how Jesus must have felt before He became the fulfilment of Passover and the feast of Unleavened Bread.

In Gethsemane, Jesus prayed, saying: *"Father, if it is Your will, take this cup away from Me; nevertheless not My will, but Yours be done"* (Luke 22:42). For Jesus, His cup did indeed run over. *'Then His sweat became like great drops of blood falling down to the ground'* (Luke 22:44). For Jesus, Gethsemane was pivotal, and so these words, **'My cup runs over'**, are included as a pivotal portrayal of Jesus (like olives) being crushed.

Psalm 23 and the Feast of Trumpets
(Leviticus 23:23–25).

The first day of the Hebrew civil year was when the Feast of Trumpets was observed and two silver trumpets were blown as: *'A memorial for you before your God: I am the LORD your God'* (Numbers 10:2 & 10).

Jewish tradition teaches that this was when Abraham took Isaac to Mount Moriah and there Abraham took the wood (that Isaac had carried on his back) and prepared an altar to offer up his son to God. As Abraham was about to slay Isaac, the angel of the LORD intervened and told Abraham not to kill his son: *'Then Abraham lifted his eyes and looked, and there behind him was a ram caught in a thicket by its horns. So Abraham went and took the ram and offered it up for a burnt offering instead of his son'* (Genesis 22:13). These two aspects remind us of how Jesus carried His cross on his back, and a crown of thorns was placed on His head.

At the Feast of Trumpets, the sound of the trumpet is a reminder that if we obey God (as Abraham obeyed God), we will be saved from death. In today's terms (like Isaac), it means being saved from the consequence of sin, which is death. The 14th stanza from Psalm 23:

'Surely goodness and mercy shall follow me.'

Silver in the Bible is often seen as a sign of redemption, and in the two silver trumpets used at the time of the

Feast of Trumpets, there is a clear representation of the gospel. The first silver trumpet I see as representing God's goodness and is illustrated in what Jesus said to the Pharisee Nicodemus: *"For God so loved the world that He gave His only begotten Son"* (John 3:16). God's goodness is seen in His love. The second silver trumpet I see as representing God's mercy, and is linked to His love by what Jesus said next: *"that whoever believes in Him should not perish but have eternal life"* (John 3:15–16). God's mercy is seen in His kindness. God's goodness and His mercy are inseparable.

Psalm 23 and the Day of Atonement
(Leviticus 23:27–32).

Once I had seen Psalm 23 has a striking resemblance to the seven Feasts of the Lord (and these portraits are given in the same sequence as they were given by God to Moses), it then became clear that the next stanza must correspond to the Day of Atonement, the holiest day of all in the Hebrew calendar. Therefore, as we read the next words from Psalm 23, we note how the day Jesus was to be born had been meticulously prepared. One's life-span consists of the day they were born to the day they die. This was also true of Jesus; for His life-span was so accurately defined in the 15th stanza of Psalm 23.

'All the days of my life.'

It was these six words which prompted me to see Jesus; from the day He was born to the day He died.

To comprehend this very nominal description of the 15th stanza of Psalm 23, is to grasp why God chose the date for the Day of Atonement – it is a *'SIGN'*.

The date set-aside for the Hebrew Day of Atonement was never a man's choice; God chose the date and He later informed Moses of His decision (to be observed forever). I am convinced God knew precisely when and where Jesus would be born, and also the time and place where He would later die.

What is so interesting about the words *'All the days of my life'* and how they describe the life-span of Jesus, is how similar words are found in Genesis chapter three. Here we read: *'The LORD God said to the serpent: "Because you have done this, you are cursed more than all cattle, and more than every beast of the field; on your belly you shall go, and you shall eat dust <u>all the days of your life</u>"'* (verse 14). To Adam, God said: *"Cursed is the ground for your sake; in toil you shall eat it <u>all the days of your life</u>"* (verse 17). God's rebuke to the serpent, and also to Adam who sinned when he disobeyed God, are so similar to the words found in Psalm 23:6 – **'All the days of my life'.**

From when He was born in Bethlehem, to when He died at Calvary, Jesus' life-span may be described by using the same words as found in Genesis 3 (then Psalm 23), that Jesus would experience when He became accursed of God by being nailed to a tree. (See Deuteronomy 21:23 and Acts 10:39).

Psalm 23 and the Feast of Tabernacles
(Leviticus 23:33–43).

The Feast of Tabernacles (*'The Feast of Ingathering'*) completes Israel's seven times of remembrance, and in the 16th stanza of Psalm 23 we read:

'And I will dwell in the house of the LORD.'

John 1:14 – *'And the Word* [Jesus] *became flesh and dwelt* [or tabernacled] *among us, and we beheld His glory, the glory as of the only begotten of the Father, full of grace and truth.'*

The appearance of Jesus was temporary, as with the *'Sukkot'* that Jewish people construct and dwell in for seven days during the Feast of Tabernacles, when their final harvest (fruits and berries) has been gathered in. Once Jesus had completed the work His Father sent Him to do (as He died, Jesus cried out: *'It is finished!'*), to gather in a harvest of people from the world He had created, Jesus was able to return to His Father and to: *'Dwell in the House of the LORD'* (Psalm 23:6 & Hebrews 12:1–2). For those who believe in Jesus and have received Him as their Saviour, they can look ahead to the end-time of ingathering and their eternal rest.

Psalm 23 and the Final Stanza

The final stanza in Psalm 23 contains only one word, yet it expresses two sentiments. The first sentiment is related to how long the Children of Israel were told to keep the seven festivals of the Lord, and so this final stanza is connected to these festivals. As it states in Psalm 23:6 (and also Exodus 23:14, Leviticus 16:34, and 23:41), God said they were to keep these festivals:

'Forever.'

The second sentiment I see as referring to the promise Jesus gave to all who put their trust in Him; everlasting life, which means, of course: **'Forever'.**

Professor H. C. Leupold, D.D.

Professor of Old Testament exegesis, H. C. Leupold D.D., of the Evangelical Lutheran Seminary of Capital University, Columbus, Ohio, in his book: *'Exposition of the Psalms'* (1959), of Psalm 23, he writes as follows.

*'One grammatical item must be noted in determining the whole pattern of the translation. Practically all versions from the Septuagint down very properly begin with the future in v.1, "I shall not want." From this point onward all the verbs till 5a have the same form of the Hebrew verb – the imperfect. Consistency demands that these imperfects be rendered either as futures or presents. Though the Hebrew verb allows for either, the future deserves the preference, for on the basis of the fact that the Lord is the shepherd, the psalmist looks confidently toward the **future**. This plain fact, though noted already in the Prayer Book Version* [Book of

Common Prayer] *has not been observed in any of the familiar versions, not even in the RSV.'*

As Professor Leupold makes clear, if all but one of the verbs in Psalm 23 indicates the future, this suggests the Psalmist was not writing about his own experience, but rather that of another. Professor Leupold also refers to other commentators who have said Psalm 23 is pitched on too high a level to be in any real sense attainable by any saint of God. Presumably this must rule out the Psalm's author, King David? But if David is not the focus of Psalm 23, then who is – if it is not Jesus?

In his conclusion of Psalm 23, Leupold, although not fully persuaded Psalm 23 is a Messianic Psalm, he does say Jesus is *'The Good Shepherd'*. Leupold also writes concerning Psalm 23: *'It suggests thoughts that point in the direction of the Messiah'*.

Is Psalm 23 a paraphrase of Leviticus 23 and the seven festivals Israel has observed since the time of Moses? I believe so. Consequently, I see Jesus as the fulfilment of these seven festivals – meaning, God as we know, was planning for our salvation, long before Jesus was born.

****

On the next two pages there are eight questions which are based on this study. The suggested answers can be found on page 223.

Study 6 Questions – Psalm 23

1. In the first two verses of Psalm 23, what type of animal might the writer be referring to?

ANSWER: _____

2. Psalm 23:3 refers to *'Paths of Righteousness'*. Of the seven Hebrew festivals, which festival might this be a description of?

ANSWER: _____

3. Psalm 23:4 refers to, *'I walk through the valley of the shadow of death'*. Where might this place have been?

ANSWER: _____

4. Psalm 23:5 refers to a table being prepared, *'In the presence of my enemies'*. When Jesus made Himself known to two of His disciples (Luke 24:28–31), what was Jesus doing when He revealed Himself to them? On which of Israel's seven times of remembrance might this day have been?

ANSWER: _____

_____

5. Psalm 23:5 refers to: *'You anoint my head with oil'.* Which (Hebrew) festival was being observed when the disciples were anointed with the Holy Spirit? (In Greek it is called Pentecost).

ANSWER: _____

6. Psalm 23:6 refers to: *'Surely goodness and mercy shall follow me'.* Describe what you know about God's goodness and His mercy.

ANSWER: _____

_____

7. Psalm 23:6 refers to: *'All the days of my life'.* What is the sixth Hebrew festival called? (Refer to Leviticus 23). How do these words describe the sacrifice offered to God on this day?

ANSWER: _____

_____

8. The Feast of Tabernacles is the last of the seven Hebrew festivals and marks the time when the final harvest is gathered in. Describe from Psalm 23, what awaits those who have served God. How long will this experience last?

ANSWER: _____

_____

STUDY 7 – HANUKKAH

The third sign that the birth of Jesus took place on the Hebrew/Jewish Day of Atonement is connected to darkness and light. *'In the beginning ... darkness was on the face of the deep'* (Genesis 1:1–2). Then God said: *"Let there be light"* (verse 3). Night-time is the most likely time when Jesus was born. *'Now there were in the same country shepherds living out in the fields, keeping watch over their flock by night'* (Luke 2:8).

In the beginning when darkness held sway, God said: *"Let there be light."* Jesus said to the Pharisees (those who were living in spiritual darkness): *"I am the light of the world. He who follows Me shall not walk in darkness, but have the light of life"* (John 8:12).

A parallel of Genesis chapter one can be found in John chapter one (notice how John commences his gospel in a similar way as Genesis commences). *'In the beginning was the Word, and the Word was with God, and the Word was God. He was in the beginning with God. All things were made through Him, and without Him nothing was made that was made. In Him was life, and the life was the light of men. And the light shines in the darkness and the darkness did not comprehend it'* (John 1:1–5). John is clearly writing about Jesus.

The next link in the chain of events is John the Baptist. Malachi wrote: *"Behold, I send My messenger, and he will prepare the way before Me. And the Lord, whom you seek, will suddenly come to His temple, even the Messenger of the covenant, in whom you delight. Behold He is coming," says the LORD of hosts. "Behold, I will send you Elijah the prophet before the coming of the great and dreadful day of the LORD. And He will turn the hearts of the fathers to the children, and the hearts of the children to their fathers, lest I come and strike the earth with a curse"* (Malachi 3:1 & 4:5–6).

The fulfilment of this prophecy is found in Matthew's Gospel, where Jesus is teaching. *"What did you go out into the wilderness to see? A reed shaken by the wind? But what did you go out to see? A man clothed in soft garments? Indeed, those who wear soft clothing are in king's houses. But what did you go out to see? A prophet? Yes, I say to you, and more than a prophet. For this is he of whom it is written: 'Behold, I send My messenger before Your face, who will prepare Your way before You'* [see Malachi 3:1]. *Assuredly, I say to you, among those born of women there has not risen one greater than John the Baptist ... and if you are willing to receive it, he is Elijah who is to come. He who has ears to hear, let him hear!"* (Matthew 11:7–15). And in John's Gospel: *'There was a man sent from God, whose name was John. This man came for a witness, to bear witness of the Light, that all through him might believe. He was not that Light but was sent to bear witness of that Light. That was the true Light which gives light to every man coming into the world'* (John 1:6–9).

God's gift of *'Light'* and John the Baptist (Elijah) are what are spoken of at the beginning and at the end of the Old Testament Scriptures; and the two are book-ends, to enable us to see something very remarkable concerning the time chosen for the birth of Jesus.

The Apocrypha

A few years after I became a believer in Jesus, I became aware of a selection of ancient Jewish writings known as the *'Apocrypha Writings'*, that Christians were not expected to read. The Apocrypha writings are not considered by most theologians (Gentiles) as inspired Scripture, and so they are not included in the majority of Bibles that Christians use. At about the same time, I learnt that there were approximately four hundred years between the closing of the Old Testament period, and the commencement of the New Testament period.

It is sad that these four hundred years of Jewish history has been overlooked by most Christians, for it is not discussed because of its non-appearance in most Bibles. However, for Jewish people, it is an important part of their history, and we know that Jesus identified Himself with this period at the Jewish festival of Hanukkah.

The Festival of Hanukkah

Only two days after I published my first booklet about the timing for the birth of Jesus (February 2011), in which I included the details of the first two signs, I purchased two Bible study books. Each author included a proposal that Jesus may have been conceived at the Jewish festival of Hanukkah. The writers then went on to explain how this would mean Jesus would have been born nine months later, during the Jewish festival of the Feast of Tabernacles. If both authors were correct (and I had no reason to suspect they were not), it meant I would have to reconsider my own conviction that Jesus was born at the time of the Jewish Day of Atonement.

It may help if I explain the background to Hanukkah. Hanukkah dates to the second century B.C.E., when Antiochus IV Epiphanies, a Syrian king, desecrated the temple in Jerusalem by erecting a statue to the pagan god Zeus. Antiochus then sacrificed pigs in the temple. Antiochus also instructed that copies of the *'Torah'*, the five books of Moses, were to be burnt. In the book of 1 Maccabees, it states that in the year 167 B.C.E., on the fifteenth day of the Hebrew month Kislev, *'Antiochus built the appalling abomination on the top of the altar of burnt offering.'* Later, *'on the twenty-fifth day of each month, sacrifice was offered on the altar erected on top of the altar of burnt offering'* (1 Maccabees 1:54 & 59).

A number of years earlier, God had informed Daniel (a prophet) this would happen, and so Daniel recorded the following prophecy. *'And forces shall be mustered by him, and they shall defile the sanctuary fortress; then they shall take away the daily sacrifices, and place there the abomination of desolation'* (Daniel 11:31).

Such sacrilege, of course, was against everything God had intended for His people, but the Children of Israel were unable to oppose it. Three years later, in 164 B.C.E., and under the leadership of a family who became known in Israel as *'The Maccabees'*, Antiochus and the Syrians were defeated and Israel's temple in Jerusalem was cleansed.

Later, *'on the twenty-fifth of the ninth month Kislev* [in 164 B.C.E.]*, they rose at dawn and offered a lawful sacrifice on the new altar of burnt offering which they had made. The altar was dedicated to the sound of hymns, zithers, lyres and cymbals, at the same time of the year and on the same day on which the Gentiles had originally profaned it'* (1 Maccabees 4:52–54).

Israel's return to lawful sacrifices would eventually become known as Hanukkah – the Festival of Lights – because on this day the menorah lamps were relit. The priests, however, had only enough purified oil to last for one day; nevertheless, tradition records the menorah lamps continued to burn for eight days before new oil could be pressed and purified. The eight-day burning of the menorah lamps from one day's supply of oil is still thought of by Jewish people as being a miracle.

Hanukkah is also known as the Feast of Dedication, and it appears Jesus participated in this feast. *'Now it was the Feast of Dedication in Jerusalem and it was winter. And Jesus walked in the temple in Solomon's porch'* (John 10:22–23).

Therefore, on what basis have some suggested Jesus was conceived at the time of Hanukkah, and born nine months later at the time of the Feast of Tabernacles?

The first author I quote from is Dr. Richard Booker, M.B.A., founder/director of the Institute for Hebraic-Christian Studies. In his book *'Celebrating Jesus in the Biblical Feasts'*, Booker writes:

'It is possible that Jesus, God's true light, was conceived during Hanukkah, the Feast of Lights. According to Luke 1:5, Zacharias was a priest of the division of Abijah. Luke 1:8–11 says that Gabriel appeared to Zacharias when he was serving as a priest in the temple. Based on Rabbinic writings, the division of Abijah served as priests during the second half of the fourth month on the Jewish religious calendar [See 1 Chronicles 24:1–19]. *It was then late June when Elizabeth conceived John the Baptist. According to Luke 1:24–26, Mary conceived Jesus in the sixth month of Elizabeth's pregnancy. This means that Jesus was conceived during the latter part of the Jewish month Kislev, or late December on the Gentile calendar. Jesus was born nine months later, most likely during the Feast of Tabernacles. Forty days after Jesus was born, He was dedicated to His heavenly Father at the temple. It was there that Simeon said that Jesus was a light to bring revelation to the Gentiles, and the glory of Israel* [Luke 2:32]. *God's true light had come into the world to reveal His Father to us.'*

The second author I quote is Dr. Jacob Keegstra (B.Sc. in Civil Engineering). With a Masters in philosophy, theology, divinity and business administration, Keegstra is the director of the Dutch branch of the International Christian Embassy, Jerusalem. Keegstra is the author of the booklet: *'God's Prophetic Feasts'*.

'We know that the priest Zacharias was serving in the temple when the angel came to him to announce the birth of John the Baptist. Zacharias was assigned to the eighth group of Abijah and served during the week of the 12th Siwan. If we add the forty weeks for a normal pregnancy, we reach the 14th Nisan; this means that John the Baptist was born at the beginning of Passover.

*'According to Judaism, the herald of the Messiah is expected in a Passover night. Jesus was born six months after John; thus we reach the Feast of Tabernacles. Nine months before this feast, the Feast of Lights takes place, which means that Jesus was presumably conceived around the Feast of Lights or Hanukkah Feast. Was Jesus, the Light of the world, conceived at the Feast of Lights? We do know that Jesus did not come by chance, but He came in the fullness of time, very consciously at God's time. **Apparently, God's acts of salvation are inseparably bound up with His festivals.'*** Keegstra's final suggestion is understandable; yet deeply profound. (Bold text is my own emphasis).

Because my booklet had been published only two days before I acquired Booker and Keegstra's books, and my research indicated Jesus was born on the Jewish Day of Atonement was now being displaced by an alternative suggestion, I decided I must do something practical – a two-hundred-and-eighty-day analysis! Two hundred and eighty days is the internationally accepted time period for the gestation of the human embryo, from the time of conception through to the time of giving birth. Two hundred and eighty days is forty weeks.

Starting, therefore, at midnight at Hanukkah (in 2011, the date was Wednesday, December 21st – the 25th day of Kislev in the Jewish lunar calendar when the temple in Jerusalem had been rededicated), I counted forward two hundred and eighty days and discovered the forty week period culminated not at the Feast of Tabernacles, but at midnight on the Jewish Day of Atonement!

In 2011, the date for the celebration of Hanukkah was Wednesday, December 21st. In 2012, the date for the observance of the Day of Atonement was Wednesday, September 26th. The time interval between these two dates was forty weeks! It was not until I considered the link between the solar calendar and the Hebrew lunar calendar, and these two ancient Jewish festivals, that I discovered it was exactly forty weeks from Hanukkah (in 2011) to the Day of Atonement (in 2012).

Soon after reading Booker and Keegstra's two books, it occurred to me that Paul wrote: *'But when the fullness of the time had come, God sent forth His Son, born of a woman, born under the law'* (Galatians 4:4).

I do not believe that when Mary reached the full-term of her pregnancy – from when the Holy Spirit had come upon her (Luke 1:35) – Mary would have gone overdue by nearly a week (the Feast of Tabernacles commences on the fifteen day of the seventh month, five days after the Day of Atonement – Leviticus 23:39). When it came to the day of His birth, I believe Jesus was born on-time, on the Day of Atonement, and forty weeks is the length of time from the festival of Hanukkah in one year, to the observance of the Day of Atonement in the following year. *'As for God, His way is perfect; the word of the LORD is proven'* (Psalm 18:30). Always!

It is beyond my ability to explain how Jesus broke through the barriers of time and space to enter the womb of Mary, a virgin, a *'SIGN'* (Isaiah 7:14), when an egg from one of her ovaries had just entered her uterus. For the foetus of God's Son to then spend forty weeks in her womb before being born as the Son of Man, is, I know, amazing, but this is what the Hebrew Foundations of the Christian Faith teaches us.

King David was probably the first to write about Mary's role in becoming the mother of Jesus. What is the most well-known Psalm providing intimate detail of the birth of the Lord Jesus, David wrote: *'But You are He who took Me out of the womb* [Mary's womb]. *You made Me trust while on My mother's breasts* [Mary's breasts]. *I was cast upon You from birth. From my mother's womb You have been My God'* (Psalm 22:9–10).

Try now to imagine Mary in a synagogue in Nazareth with her six-month old infant in her arms, as she listens to one of the local Rabbis reading this same Psalm (22). Might she have thought: *"That's my womb and my breasts King David is referring to."* But as the Rabbi continues with his reading, Mary hears him say: *'They pierced My hands and My feet; I can count all My bones. They look and stare at Me. They divide My garments among them, and for My clothing they cast lots'* (Psalm 22:16–18). What would have been Mary's thoughts then? Of course we do not know, but Psalm 22 anticipates the personal anguish Mary was to experience thirty-three years later as she watched her Son suffer and die when he was nailed to a Roman cross.

At such a difficult time, might Mary have looked back to when Gabriel visited her, six months after Elizabeth had conceived, conscious that what had taken place in her womb had been a miracle? I'm sure Mary would not forget Gabriel's visit, and although at times she may have been confused, Mary would have known her Son was unique; but more than this, and at this time of Passover, He was her Saviour; Israel's Messiah.

****

On the next two pages there are six questions which are based on this study. The suggested answers can be found on page 224.

Study 7 Questions – Hanukkah

1. List three statements from Genesis 1:1–5 and John 1:1–5 which are similar.

ANSWER: _____

_____

_____

_____

_____

_____

2. Who is the *'Messenger/Prophet'* spoken of in Malachi 3:1 and 4:5–6? (See also Mathew 11:7–15).

ANSWER: _____

3. Hanukkah, an ancient Hebrew festival, marks the time when the Syrians were defeated through the leadership of a family who became known as *'The Maccabees'*. From John 10:22, we know Jesus went up to Jerusalem to keep this festival. How does John describe this festival – its name?

ANSWER: _____

4. Some writers have said Jesus could have been conceived at the time of Hanukkah. What is the internationally recognised time period for the gestation of the human embryo?

ANSWER: _____

5. In 2011, on Wednesday, December 21st, the Hebrew festival of Hanukkah was observed. Nine months later, on Wednesday, September 26th (2012), the Hebrew Day of Atonement was observed. The time interval between these two dates was exactly 280 days. How many weeks is this?

ANSWER: _____ _____

6. There may be times when we do not understand what is happening around us, or to us. However, we are still encouraged to put our trust in God. In Psalm 18:30, what did David say about God and His ways?

ANSWER: _____

_____

_____

****

STUDY 8 – OUR HIGH PRIEST

There are many Scriptures that focus on the Hebrew Day of Atonement, and so next we turn to the book of Hebrews. Hebrews explains how Jesus became what Israel's high priest was appointed for – the Children of Israel's intermediary in God's presence.

The book of Hebrews can be read in less than an hour and I recommend reading it in a single session as this is the best way to understand what the writer is describing. Hebrews explains Jesus as fulfilling the role of God's chosen intermediary; as Paul the apostle also taught: *'It is Christ who died, and furthermore is also risen, who is even at the right hand of God, who also makes intercession for us'* (Romans 8:34).

In His appointment as High Priest, Jesus did not enter His Father's presence with the blood of bulls and goats, but with His own blood – *"For the life of the flesh is in the blood, and I have given it to you upon the altar to make atonement for your souls; for it is the blood that makes atonement for the soul"* (Leviticus 17:11).

In Israel's ancient community, the role of the high priest was crucial, because his primary function was to act as the people's representative before God. In doing so, he performed a range of duties in order that the Children of Israel might live according to God's instructions.

Included in his various duties was one which was of far greater importance than all his other tasks. On the Day of Atonement, the high priest would not have worn his regular priestly robes; instead, he would have dressed himself in a one-piece linen garment before entering the holy-of-holies. It is likely he would have also removed his footwear – as Moses did at the burning bush.

For the high priest's first entry into the holy-of-holies, he took blood from a bull as a covering for his own sin and the sin of his family (Leviticus 16:11). Afterwards, for his second entry into the holy-of-holies, he took blood from one of two young goats as a covering for the sins of the people (verse 15). The high priest was instructed to sprinkle the blood of the sacrifice on the mercy seat, the covering of the Ark of the Covenant, and he was told to carry out this procedure on just one day a year; on the Day of Atonement.

Israel's observance was, of course, only transitory. A time would eventually arrive when God would send His Son and men and women would no longer be dependent on a priest who was restricted by his humanity – until his death – when another priest would be appointed to succeed him. Jesus is mankind's final High Priest (in Hebrew He is known as *'Cohen Gadol'*), a High Priest who continues to serve others.

The following is taken from the Complete Jewish Bible. *'But when the Messiah appeared as Cohen Gadol of the good things that are happening already, then, through the greater and more perfect Tent which is not man-made [that is, not of this created world] he entered the Holiest Place once and for all. And he entered not by means of the blood of goats and calves, but by means of his own blood, thus setting people free forever'* (Hebrews 9:11–12).

The specific mention in this passage of goats and calves and Jesus entering the *'Holiest Place once and for all'*, indicates the writer is recalling what took place on the Day of Atonement, and not the other occasions when the high priest performed his duties in the tabernacle. In the book of Revelation, it states: *'Then the temple of God was opened in heaven, and the ark of His covenant was seen in His temple'* (Revelation 11:19).

The tabernacle – *'The Tent of Meeting'* – which was made by Moses in the wilderness was not an original, but a copy of the temple in heaven as seen by John. Therefore, the Ark of the Covenant is a connecting link between the holy-of-holies in the tent of meeting, and the temple of God in heaven.

When writing about Jesus in the book of Hebrews, the writer frequently refers to Jesus as our High Priest, and so these next words are very telling: *'So also Christ did not glorify Himself to become high priest, but it was He who said to Him: "You are My Son, today I have begotten You"'* (Hebrews 5:5).

What is fascinating about this verse is how it is rendered in the Complete Jewish Bible; but first we must see its context. Aaron served as a priest, and one of his many tasks was to go into the holy-of-holies on the Day of Atonement to meet with God – as God likewise visited the holy-of-holies on this same day (Leviticus 16:2).

For those who count themselves as God's people, they should always be: *'looking unto Jesus, the author and finisher of our faith, who for the joy that was set before Him endured the cross, despising the shame, and has sat down at the right hand of God'* (Hebrews 12:2).

This, then, is how Hebrews 5:5 is given in the Complete Jewish Bible. *'Neither did the Messiah glorify himself to become Cohen Gadol* [High Priest]; *rather, it was the One who said to Him, "You are My Son; today I have become Your Father."'* The question for the reader is naturally this: *"Which 'Today' is God is referring to?"*

This acknowledgment in Hebrews 5:5 (quoted also in Hebrews 1:5, in the context that at the time of His birth, Jesus was and is the express image of God) is a direct quote from Psalm 2. Psalm 2 (as with Psalms 22, 23, and 24) is a Psalm that refers to Jesus. So when the Psalmist says: *'Today'*, which day is he referring to? I believe it to be the Day of Atonement, for this is the day God told Moses that the high priest was to enter the holy-of-holies and for him to make an atonement sacrifice for the sins of God's people.

The timing for the birth of Jesus was very much in-line with the high priest's duty on the Day of Atonement, when he entered the holy-of-holies to make atonement for the sins of God's people; for he carried out this task every year on the tenth day of the seventh month.

The birth of Jesus heralded Him as being: *'Immanuel, God with us'*, and His appearance from heaven and His entry into this world was in order for Him to become a substitute at Passover – Passover occurring exactly half a solar year after the Day of Atonement. The principle for the Day of Atonement to occur half a solar year before Passover is one that is enshrined in Scripture.

Twenty-five years after the Children of Israel were taken by Nebuchadnezzar into captivity to Babylon, Ezekiel experienced, *'The hand of the LORD'* being laid upon him and taking him in the power of the Spirit back to the land of Israel. The date God laid His hand upon Ezekiel was the tenth day of the first month (Ezekiel 40:1–3). It was the date set-aside for the priests to select a lamb without blemish for Passover. (It seems within the Hebrew calendar, the tenth day of the first month – the selection of a lamb for Passover – and the tenth day of the seventh month – the Day of Atonement – both are very important). As part of Ezekiel's vision (which is described over nine chapters, 40–48), and included in God's instructions to Ezekiel, there exists a pattern for worship that is to be followed closely on all the Lord's appointed feast days (His days of remembrance).

Ezekiel was instructed: *"But when the people of the land come before the LORD on the appointed feast days, whoever enters by way of the north gate to worship shall go out by way of the south gate; and whoever enters by way of the south gate shall go out by way of the north gate. He shall not return by way of the gate through which he came, but shall go out through the opposite gate. The prince shall then be in their midst. When they go in, he shall go in and when they go out he shall go out"* (Ezekiel 46:9–10).

In His message to Ezekiel, God gave instructions as to how His people should approach Him. *"Whoever enters by way of the north gate to worship; should go out by the south gate, and whoever goes in by way of the south gate to worship; should leave by the north gate."* When God's people approach God, they must not leave by turning around and walking away, but to go out in the opposite direction. This reminds us of what happened to Lot's wife, when she disobeyed the angel by looking back to Sodom, a city of bestial immorality.

The principle still applies; whatever we left when we came to God, we should not look back. The apostle Paul testified to his own commitment: *'I press toward the goal for the prize of the upward call of God in Christ Jesus'* (Philippians 3:14), and not to return to former things that might hold him back. The procedure is seen in what Paul explained should happen when we present ourselves to God. *'When I was a child, I spoke as a child, I understood as a child, I thought as a child; but when I became a man, I put away childish things. For now we see in a mirror dimly, but then face to face'* (1 Corinthians 13:11–12).

My reasoning for the fourth sign for Jesus' birth is, I do admit, basic. As Israel's high priest was preparing to enter the holy-of-holies on the Day of Atonement, Jesus was born. For me, it seems the most logical explanation.

'Harmony in Opposites' abound in Scripture, as they do in real life. For example – *'Then the LORD said in His heart, "While the earth remains, seedtime and harvest, cold and heat, winter and summer, and day and night shall not cease"'* (Genesis 8:21–22). Marriage was designed for procreation to take place when male and female – opposites – become one flesh (Genesis 2:24).

'Therefore in all things He [Jesus] *had to be made like His brethren, that He might be a merciful and faithful high priest in things pertaining to God'* (Hebrews 2:17). The priesthood of Jesus was in keeping with what went before, for Israel's high priest was an antitype of Jesus.

Bethlehem was a pragmatic choice for the birth-place of Jesus, for it was here the shepherds who looked after the Passover lambs were informed of His birth. *'But you, Bethlehem Ephrathah, though you are little among the thousands of Judah, yet out of you shall come forth to Me the One to be Ruler in Israel, whose goings forth are from of old, from everlasting'* (Micah 5:2).

Equally pragmatic was the day chosen for the birth of Jesus. The Day of Atonement was entirely appropriate, for it featured the reason which pointed to His birth – the recurring duty of Israel's high priest.

The birth of Jesus was a joyous event, but later, when Jesus died at the time of Passover, it was a cruel event; nevertheless, the two events were necessary, because for Jesus there was: *'A time to be born and a time to die'* (Ecclesiastes 3:2). Concisely: *'All the days of His life'*.

For God to send Jesus and for His birth to occur as the high priest was preparing to enter the purity of the holy-of-holies (like an embryo in a womb), fitted the pattern of God's divine order. However, the high priest's entry was imperfect, because of his frailty and his propensity to commit sin. Only Jesus could have provided a perfect solution to the problem of man's sin, and so the thought of His birth on the Day of Atonement is (to my mind) entirely appropriate.

Historically, Israel's appointed times suggests there is no other day in the annual cycle of their calendar that would appear as being suitable for the birth of Jesus, other than on the Day of Atonement. If not the Day of Atonement, then why did God set this day aside?

It is inconceivable Jesus would have ignored the Day of Atonement, for He knew He had been appointed to act as our intermediary; the One who came from the real Holy-of-Holies and who would one day return.

The apostle Paul wrote that Jesus became *'A servant to the circumcision'* (Romans 15:8). In becoming a servant to the Jews, Jesus would have identified Himself in every way with the promises made by God to Israel, for the veracity of Scripture depended on it. Shortly before He was crucified, Jesus said to His disciples: *"I came forth from the Father and have come into the world. Again, I leave the world and go to the Father"* (John 16:28). These words recall His relationship with His Father, but they also recall His birth and His death.

It is most unlikely the date chosen for Jesus' birth was not important to God. God knew that from when Jesus was born, His destiny was to become our High Priest, and His ministry would commence from when He reached age thirty (Numbers 4). Three-and-a-half years later (Daniel 9:27), Jesus became a Passover sacrifice.

From when God witnessed the death of His Son, He knew that for those who put their trust in Him, they would not be condemned to eternal death and separation from God. Jesus came to bring us freedom from being slaves to sin and sin's consequences.

The book of Hebrews is a very dependable book, for it acts as a hinge between the Old and New Testaments. In Hebrews we read: *'Seeing then that we have a great high priest who has passed through the heavens, Jesus the Son of God, let us hold fast our confession. For we do not have a high priest who cannot sympathize with our weaknesses, but was in all points tempted as we are, yet without sin. Let us therefore come boldly to the throne of grace, that we may obtain mercy and find grace to help in time of need'* (Hebrews 4:14–16). The *'Let us'* (plural), recalls what God said when He made man on the sixth day: *'Let Us make man in Our image, according to Our likeness'* (Genesis 1:26).

Priestly Garments

When I spotted *'Carta's Illustrated Encyclopedia of the Holy Temple in Jerusalem'* in a bookshop in Tel Aviv, I knew it was worth the forty pounds cover price. It was here I read that for the priests who served in the Temple, their priestly garments are not sewn like other clothes; each item is woven, seamless, of one piece.

In John we read as Jesus was dying, the soldiers who had crucified Him, *'took His garments and made four parts, to each soldier a part, and also the tunic. Now the tunic was without seam, woven from the top in one piece. They said therefore among themselves, "Let us not tear it, but cast lots for it, whose it shall be", that the Scripture might be fulfilled which says: "They divided My garments among them, and for my clothing they cast lots"'* (John 19:23–24, quoting Psalm 22:18). His one-piece tunic confirms that Jesus was sent by God to become, for those who believe in Him, their High Priest.

In his book, *'Hope for the Nations'*, Tom Holland writes: *'The theme of Jesus being the believers' high priest is not limited to the letter to the Hebrews as some think; it is present throughout the gospels and the rest of the New Testament.'*

THE LORD'S DAY OF ATONEMENT

Attention to detail is one of the Bible's hallmarks, and in the ancient book of Hebrews, we read twice (quoting Psalm 2:7), *'You are My Son, today I have become Your Father'* (Hebrews 1:5 & 5:5).

Such indication, surely, must point to a day, chosen by God, for when Mary was to give birth? If true, might it not also recall when God met with Aaron in the tent of meeting's holy-of-holies, when the two of them came together on the Day of Atonement? In Leviticus chapter sixteen, we read that the Lord said to Moses: *"for I will appear in the cloud above the mercy seat"* (Leviticus 16:2). Does this not suggest that this day may also be described as: *'THE LORD'S DAY OF ATONEMENT'* ?

Within the biblical setting, Jesus' birth and the Day of Atonement should not be seen as a co-incidence, but rather, part of the Hebrew Foundations of the Christian Faith that has existed since the time of Moses.

****

On the next two pages there are seven questions which are based on this study. The suggested answers can be found on page 225.

Study 8 Questions – Our High Priest

1. In Romans 8:34, we read that Jesus is now at the right hand of God. What is He doing?

ANSWER: _____

2. In Israel's ancient community, the role of the high priest was crucial. What is the role of those who have surrendered their lives to God?

ANSWER: _____

_____

3. Hebrews 1:3 refers to Jesus as having, *'Sat down at the right hand of the Majesty on high.'* What did Jesus do before He sat down?

ANSWER: _____

_____

4. Hebrews 9:11–12 refers to Jesus as having entered: *'Not with the blood of goats and calves, but with His own blood He entered'*. Where did Jesus enter?

ANSWER: _____

_____

5. The mention of goats and calves in Hebrew 9:12 recalls the type of sacrifice Jewish people would have offered on one of their seven appointed times of remembrance. According to Leviticus 23:27, it was a holy convocation. What was the name given to this time of remembrance?

ANSWER: _____

6. We know, *'Christ did glorify Himself to become high priest, but it was He* [God] *who said to Him...'* Complete this statement (Hebrews 5:5).

ANSWER: _____

_____

7. The answer to the previous question quotes a prophecy from Psalm 2. From this prophecy – quoted also in Hebrews 1:5 where we read of God saying: *'I will be to Him a Father, and He shall be to Me a Son'* – it appears a certain day is being referred to for the birth of God's Son.

   1. Do you think this day was important to God?

   2. Do you think this day should be important to those who believe in God?

ANSWER: 1. _____ 2. _____

THE FIRST AND THE LAST

Before we consider Study Nine – the first book and the first chapter – I would like to refer to the last book in the Bible and the last chapter. Here we read of how Jesus understood His authority: *'I am the Alpha and the Omega, the Beginning and the End, the First and the Last'* (Revelation 22:13).

The first chapter in the Bible recalls the first miracle Jesus performed, when like His Father who spoke the *'Word'* to bring about Creation, Jesus, who is *'The Word of God'* (Revelation 19:13), also spoke the *'Word'*. The miracle concerned a lack of wine at a wedding ceremony (John 2:1–11). Not only was this the *first* miracle Jesus performed, it also concerned the *last* of the wine which was to be consumed at the wedding.

Did Jesus see His appearance at this wedding was to depict Himself at the *'Marriage Supper of the Lamb'* (Revelation 19), when God will wipe away all tears and there will be no more death (Revelation 21:4)? Was it intended that what took place at this wedding, that the miracle was to portray the *'Beginning of Days'* when God made us for Himself – as His companions – and the *'End of Days'*, when Jesus will be revealed as the Bridegroom of Heaven? If so, then perhaps this final study will begin to unravel some of the mystery of these beginning and end-time events.

STUDY 9 – CREATION WEEK

What I have sought to do in these studies is to explore some of the Hebrew Foundations of the Christian Faith. That I have paid particular attention to the birth-day of Jesus (Studies 5–8) has been deliberate, for His birth was when He became human. To remember His birth at Christmas can result in His birth becoming opaque, for its content for many is pagan, rather than Hebraic.

Just two days before Jesus died, He said: *"O Jerusalem, Jerusalem, the one who kills the prophets and stones those who are sent to her! How often I wanted to gather your children together, as a hen gathers her chicks under her wings, but you were not willing!"* (Matthew 23:37). Jesus likened Himself to a hen, who when faced with danger will do her utmost to protect her new-born from predators, even if it means death. Her wings are her way of protecting her young, a type of atonement.

Was Jesus thinking about Ezekiel 16? Here we read of Jerusalem being described as a new-born baby whose naval cord was not cut, not washed with water, nor wrapped in *'swaddling cloths'*, but thrown into a field, struggling in its own blood (Ezekiel 16:1–6). However, for Jerusalem there is hope, for at the end of this critique we read: *"Then you shall know that I am the LORD ... when I provide you an atonement* [in swaddling cloths?] *for all you have done"* (verses 62 & 63).

This passage recalls the final words from the Song of Moses; a song written by God (Deuteronomy 31:19). *"He* [God] *will provide atonement for His land and His people"* (Deuteronomy 32:43). The work of atonement (which is linked to the Day of Atonement), is how Jews and Gentiles can be re-united with God.

When Adam and Eve sinned, and hid because they were ashamed of their nakedness, God killed an animal to provide them with a covering. Because we, too, have inherited a sinful nature, is why we are in need of God's covering; as seen in the first day of atonement sacrifice that was performed in the Garden of Eden (Genesis 3:21). The meaning of atonement is: *'To Cover'*.

As I thought about Israel's seven festivals of the Lord (Leviticus 23), I was puzzled as to why Passover came first (the death of Jesus), and what was the significance of the *order* of these times? (And so I prayed). On Wednesday, January 23rd 2013, at about 4:30 p.m., I asked Janet (my wife) if she would like a cup of tea. Her reply was: *'Yes please'*, and so I filled the kettle. In the silence of the moment, brief though it was, I felt an urge to read Genesis chapter one. Until that day, I could not say with any certainty I understood the first account of creation, but now as I read, I began to see Jesus portrayed in the world's oldest portrait, the greatest non-fiction story ever told. It has been a most memorable spiritual journey. Scales have been removed from my previous innocence of this remarkable story.

The First Day of Creation and Passover

'In the beginning God created the heavens and the earth. The earth was without form and void; and darkness was on the face of the deep. And the Spirit of God was hovering over the face of the waters. Then God said: "Let there be light"; and there was light. And God saw the light, that it was good; and God divided the light from the darkness. God called the light Day, and the darkness He called Night. So the evening and the morning were the first day' (Genesis 1:1–5).

The events of the first day (of creation) may not be as simple as first thought. For example, what is the nature of its light? Clearly it is not the light of the sun, for the sun does not feature until the fourth day.

Could this be a way of describing not only what took place at the beginning of time, but also what takes place at the end of time (*'The First and the Last'*), when the New Jerusalem, the Holy City, has *'no need of the sun or of the moon to shine in it, for the glory of God illuminated it. The Lamb is its light'* (Revelation 21:1–2 & 23)? But also, might this be a way of describing how the *'Lamb of God'* (the Lord Jesus), who is the *'Light of God'*, triumphs over the forces of spiritual darkness?

Consider now the prescribed order of the Lord's seven appointed times (Leviticus 23). Passover is described as being the first of these seven times (they are also known as *'The Lord's Seven Times of Remembrance'*).

Prior to when the Children of Israel were delivered from slavery in Egypt, Moses was told to instruct the people to select a one-year old male lamb (or goat) on the tenth day of the first month (Exodus 12:1–2). Four days later, the day of preparation for the Passover, the Passover lamb was slain and its blood smeared on the doorposts and the lintel of each house as a sign the house was occupied by God's people, and that when the Lord passed-over Egypt at midnight (a time of darkness) (Exodus 12:29), those in the house would be spared.

When Jesus entered Jerusalem – also on the tenth of the first month (John 12:1–12) – it was because at Passover He would become the *'Lamb of God'* who would take away the sins of the world; and so Jesus, *'The Light of the World'*, is linked to the first day and the first feast.

The night before He died, Jesus prayed: *"And now O Father, glorify Me together with Yourself, with the glory which I had with You before the world was … for You loved Me before the foundation of the world"* (John 17:5 & 24). Jesus knew His earthly life was soon to end.

In John's first letter we read: *'God is light and in Him is no darkness at all'* (1 John 1:5). What is described as having taken place on the first day is an indication of one of the virtues of God's character (and also of Jesus). When light appeared on the first day it displaced the darkness, because God is not characterized by darkness. Jesus said: *"I am the light of the world. He who follows me shall not walk in darkness but shall have the light of life"* (John 8:12).

Recalling how Jesus is being referred to symbolically on the first day, the night before the Light of the World was about to be *extinguished* at Passover, Jesus explained to His disciples what was about to happen to Him. *"A little while longer the light is with you. Walk while you have the light, lest darkness overtake you; he who walks in darkness does not know where he is going. While you have the light, believe in the light, that you may become sons of light"* (John 12:35–36).

The next day, when Jesus was suffering, *'there was darkness over all the earth until the ninth hour'* (Luke 23:44). It was a return to the darkness which had existed prior to God saying: *"Let there be light."* The death of Jesus at Passover completed the first event in the cycle of God's seven appointed times – or His *'Times of Remembrance'* – and so His death at Passover brought about a return to the darkness – but only briefly.

The darkness which occurred as the Light of the World was being extinguished; lasted for three hours. At the time, although the darkness was feared by those who were its witnesses (Matthew 27:54), it was not a darkness which would last forever. Because the life of Jesus was being drained from Him, is why the darkness returned. The events of the first day of creation explain Calvary at the time of Passover; for it was a reversal of the typology – once again, *'Harmony in Opposites'*. As the *'Light of the World'* was being cut off from the land of the living (Isaiah 53:8), so the darkness returned.

The Second Day and the Feast of Unleavened Bread

'Then God said, "Let there be a firmament in the midst of the waters, and let it divide the waters from the waters." Thus God made the firmament, and divided the waters which were under the firmament from the waters which were above the firmament; and it was so. And God called the firmament heaven. So the evening and the morning were the second day' (Genesis 1:6–8).

In Hebrew consciousness, two indicates separation, or division, for it is the first number which can be divided. On the second day, God divided the waters by means of a firmament, which He called Heaven. Later, Jesus taught His disciples there is separation/division between those who believe in God, and those who do not.

When God created man, He gave him two choices – to obey or not to obey – and as a consequence there are two destinies. Man's freedom to choose is related to what God did on the second day, and separation, or division, is what Jewish people do when they observe the feast of Unleavened Bread, when they remove all traces of leaven (or yeast) from their homes; for leaven is symbolic of sin, and sin can lead to wrongdoing. In a similar way to what happens when you add leaven to bread flour, habitual sin can permeate a person's life.

The second feast (Unleavened Bread) corresponds to the division God established on the second day, the division of the waters; as God later repeated for the Children of Israel to enable them to cross the Red Sea on dry land, following their four hundred years of slavery in Egypt (Genesis 15:13 & Acts 7:6).

In His Sermon on the Mount, Jesus spoke of two gates. *"Enter by the narrow gate; for wide is the gate and broad the way that leads to destruction, and there are many who go in by it. Because narrow is the gate and difficult is the way which leads to life, and there are few who find it"* (Matthew 7:13–14). The second day and the second feast, Unleavened Bread, explains why Jesus had to die; the righteous for the unrighteous.

Paul in his first letter to believers in Corinth explained this (essential) need for division: *'Do you not know that a little leaven leavens the whole lump? Therefore, purge out the old leaven, that you may be a new lump, since you truly are unleavened. For indeed Christ, our Passover, was sacrificed for us. Therefore let us keep the feast, not with the old leaven, nor with the leaven of malice and wickedness, but with the unleavened bread of sincerity and truth'* (1 Corinthians 5:6–8).

The Third Day and the Feast of Firstfruits

From Mathew 12:40, we read that Jesus rose from the dead, three days and three nights after He was crucified. His resurrection corresponded with what took place on the third day: *'Then God said, "Let the waters under the heavens be gathered together into one place, and let the dry land appear"; and it was so. And God called the dry land Earth, and the gathering together of the waters He called Seas. And God saw that it was good. Then God said. "Let the earth bring forth grass, the herb that yields seed, and the fruit tree that yields fruit according to its kind, whose seed is in itself, on the earth"; and it was so. And the earth brought forth grass, the herb that yields seed according to its kind, and the tree that yields fruit, whose seed is in itself according to its kind. And God saw that it was good. So the evening and the morning were the third day'* (Genesis 1: 9–13).

Three days after the beginning, when the earth was without form, God created life. For some, the events of the third day – the appearance of plants producing seed and fruit, prior to the appearance of the sun and the moon which control the Earth's seasons – may seem unlikely, but not if they are anticipating the resurrection of Jesus after He spent three days and nights in a tomb.

Jesus said: *"I am the resurrection and the life, He who believes in Me, though he may die, he shall live"* (John 11:25). Jesus later confirmed He was the resurrection by rising from the dead, three days and three nights after He had died. The resurrection of Jesus is most likely to have taken place at the time of the third Jewish festival, the Feast of Firstfruits, for the third day in the first week was the first time that first-fruits were observed.

Some may see a reason to query the Bible's account (order) of creation, that first-fruits occurred before the sun, moon and stars appeared on the next day.

Botanists, those who study the science of plants, know of the need for photosynthesis. Photosynthesis is the building up of certain compounds in the chlorophyll process which can only take place by means of energy provided by light. Usually it is the sun. Therefore, how can grasses and trees bear seed and fruit on the third day, before the sun and moon make their appearance on the fourth day? Such events are not so unlikely; that is, not if they are anticipating the resurrection of Jesus.

The Bible states that as Jesus was dying, it became dark. The darkness, which lasted for three hours, may be an indication that although Jesus had died, His death would not result in an enduring darkness, but that when Jesus rose from the dead, a type of photosynthesis took place by which Jesus is able to give life and purpose to those who believe in Him, for them to bear fruit, such as when the grasses and the trees bore fruit on the third day.

Three is recognized in Scripture as the number denoting resurrection, and affirms why Jesus needed to remain in the tomb for a total of three days and three nights before rising from the dead. Jesus Himself confirmed this. *"As Jonah was three days and three nights in the belly of the great fish; so will the Son of Man be three days and three nights in the heart of the earth"* (Matthew 12:40).

It was on the third day that God gathered the seas, next the dry land – the same period and sequence that Jonah was in the sea, and Jesus was in the tomb (dry land).

Arthur Walkington Pink, in his teaching about creation, in his book *'Gleanings in Genesis'* (1951), writes:

'In the third day's work our Lord's resurrection is typically set forth. Beyond doubt, that which is foreshadowed on the third day's work is resurrection. Not on the second, not on the fourth, but on the third day was life seen upon the barren earth! Perfect is the type for all who have eyes to see. Wonderfully pregnant are the words, "Let the earth bring forth" to all who have ears to hear. It was on the third day that our Lord rose again from the dead "According to the Scriptures." According to what Scriptures? Do we not have in these 9th and 11th verses of Genesis 1, the first of these Scriptures, the primitive picture of our Lord's resurrection?' The Feast of Firstfruits confirms this.

The Fourth Day and the Feast of Weeks

'Then God said, "Let there be lights in the firmament of the heavens to divide the day from the night; and let them be for signs and seasons, and for days and years; and let them be for lights in the firmament of the heavens to give light on the earth"; and it was so. Then God made two great lights; the greater light to rule the day, and the lesser light to rule the night. He made the stars also. God set them in the firmament of the heavens

to give light on the earth, and to rule over the day and over the night, and to divide the light from the darkness. And God saw that it was good. So the evening and the morning were the fourth day' (Genesis 1:14–19).

It is the sun which gives light and heat during the day, the moon which gives light and beauty at night, plus the earth's twenty-three degree tilt from its vertical axis, which governs the four seasons, and because of this, the seasons provide us (and all of God's creatures) with our food – for without it we would perish.

On the fourth day, the series of permutations that are necessary for life to exist were established, and since time immemorial, without so much as a blink of the eye, many take God's gift of food for granted.

The harvest is God's provision, and in order for the harvest to take place there is a need for the four seasons. Each season has a role to play in ensuring the harvest, and the seasons were fixed, not on the first day, but on the fourth day, when the sun and the moon appeared.

Jesus taught: *"The kingdom of God is as if a man should scatter seed on the ground, and should sleep by night and rise by day* [darkness followed by light]*, and the seed should sprout and grow, he himself does not know how. For the earth yields crops by itself: first the blade, then the head, after that the full grain in the head. But when the grain ripens, immediately he puts in the sickle, because the harvest has come"* (Mark 4:26–29).

Jesus said the Kingdom of God is like a harvest field, and the harvest is only made possible by the appearance of the sun and the moon (on the fourth day). The fourth Hebrew feast – the Feast of Weeks – is when Jewish people give thanks for their wheat harvest. It is also the time when Jesus sent the Holy Spirit to His disciples in Jerusalem, that they might become workers in the world He had created. Jesus said to them: *"The harvest is truly plentiful, but the laborers are few. Therefore pray the Lord of the harvest to send out laborers into His harvest"* (Matthew 9:37–38).

Jesus' commission was for His disciples to: *"Go into all the world and preach the gospel to every creature. He who believes and is baptized will be saved; but he who does not believe will be condemned"* (Mark 16:15–16). However, the disciples were told to wait until they had been filled with the Holy Spirit. Jesus said to them: *"Behold, I send the Promise of My Father upon you; but tarry in the city of Jerusalem until you are endued with power from on high"* (Luke 24:49).

For Jewish people, their Feast of Weeks is observed seven Sabbaths (or weeks) and one day (a total of fifty days) after their observance of the Feast of Firstfruits. In the Greek, the Feast of Weeks is called Pentecost.

When the disciples were baptised with the Holy Spirit at the time of the Feast of Weeks (Pentecost), about one hundred and twenty were in the upper room (Acts 1:15).

When Solomon dedicated the first temple in Jerusalem, one hundred and twenty priests sounded their trumpets and gave praise and thanks to God and said: *"For He is good, for His mercy endures forever"* (2 Chronicles 5:12–13). It was then that: *'the glory of the LORD filled the house of God'* (verse 14).

This *'Glory of the LORD'* which filled the house of God in Solomon's days, was so similar to what took place on the day of Pentecost – and in the same city, Jerusalem!

When Peter preached his first sermon on the day of Pentecost, he quoted from the book of the prophet Joel regarding what he and the disciples had experienced. *"But this is what was spoken by the prophet Joel: And it shall come to pass in the last days, says God, that I will pour out my Spirit on all flesh"* (Acts 2:16–17).

Continuing with his quotation, Peter said: *"I will show wonders in heaven above and signs in the earth beneath; blood and fire and vapor of smoke. The sun shall be turned into darkness and the moon into blood, before the coming of the great and awesome day of the LORD"* (Acts 2:19–20). Although Peter referred to the sun and the moon, he did not quote Joel's prophecy in full, for had he done so, he would have said: *"The threshing floors will be full of wheat and the vats shall overflow with new wine and oil"* (Joel 2:24). Joel's prophecy links Israel's wheat harvest with the sun and the moon, which were to act as *'SIGNS'* (Genesis 1:14).

In fulfillment of the *'SIGNS'* of Genesis 1:14 (the sun, moon and stars continue to give light on the earth), God's plan continues to unfold. The events which took place on the fourth day, and the command of Jesus to His disciples to wait until they had received the Holy Spirit, are simply details of God's plan first revealed in Genesis chapter one; then finally described in the last chapter of John's Revelation, where Jesus is quoted as saying: *"I am the Alpha and the Omega, the Beginning and the End, the First and the Last"* (Revelation 22:13). Designed by God, it is a plan that only He could bring to completion, through His Son the Lord Jesus.

The Fifth Day and the Feast of Trumpets

'On the fifth day God said: "Let the waters abound with an abundance of living creatures, and let birds fly above the earth across the face of the firmament of the heavens." So God created great sea creatures and every living thing that moves, with which the waters abounded, according to their kind, and every winged bird according to its kind. And God saw that it was good. And God blessed them, saying, "Be fruitful and multiply, and fill the waters in the seas, and let birds multiply on the earth." So the evening and the morning were the fifth day' (Genesis 1:20–23).

Five in Jewish thought and understanding is the number for grace; God's goodness and His mercy (Psalm 23:6). On day five, God created the sea creatures and the birds.

Can you imagine the seas and the rivers, our fields and our gardens, without them? Sea creatures and birds, their colours and their songs, provide so much pleasure and enjoyment, and they appeared on the fifth day.

The fifth of the seven appointed times, the Feast of Trumpets (in Hebrew *'Rosh HaShana'*), is observed in the Hebrew calendar on the first day of the seventh month. Some observers have suggested its purpose is to prepare God's people for the arrival nine days later of the most awesome day of all, the Day of Atonement.

The gospel is *'Good News'* because it explains God's love and His kindness, for it was designed to bring hope to a lost and dying world.

In some countries today, people are being oppressed by acts of violence and terrorism which have caused many to flee their homes (and many are dying) but can you imagine this world without any hope because there was no lovingkindness? The apostle Paul wrote: *'I am not ashamed of the gospel of Christ, for it is the power of God to salvation for everyone who believes, for the Jew first and also the Greek'* (Romans 1:16). The gospel is indeed *'Good News'*, for Jew and Gentile alike, for all who believe and put their trust in Jesus.

When God blessed the sea creatures and the birds, He then said to them: *"Be fruitful and multiply, and fill the waters in the seas, and let birds multiply on the earth"* (Genesis 1:22). God's command to the sea creatures and to the birds, to fill the seas and the earth, mirrors the last command Jesus gave to His disciples: *"Go therefore and make disciples of all the nations, baptizing them in the name of the Father and of the Son and of the Holy Spirit"* (Matthew 28:19).

Using a similar idiom to what God *first* said to the sea creatures and to the birds on the fifth day to multiply, Jesus told His disciples to make disciples in the nations. Specifically, His *last* command was for His disciples to be, *"Witnesses of Me in Jerusalem, and in Judea and Samaria, and to the end of the earth"* (Acts 1:8). The purpose for these two commands – *the first and the last* – can be found in Psalm 96:3. *'Declare His glory among the nations, His wonders among all peoples.'*

The Gospel is Preached to the Gentiles

We do not know when Peter visited Cornelius, a Roman Centurion who sent for Peter because an angel appeared to him (Acts 10). However, what we do know is Peter's visit may have been at (or near) the time of the Feast of Trumpets, the fifth feast. Consider the following.

1. An angel said to Cornelius: *"Send for Simon whose surname is Peter."* The angel's command pioneered the way for the gospel to be preached to the Gentiles.

2. The angel informed Cornelius that Peter, God's servant, was lodging in a house near to the sea.

Does this not remind us of the sea creatures God created and commanded on the fifth day to fill the rivers and the oceans?

3. Before the messengers arrived where Peter was lodging, Peter's vision included birds. Birds were the creatures who God had commanded on the fifth day to fill the earth.

4. Cornelius was known as a Gentile who feared God and one who had a good reputation with the Jews. Because of this, God knew Cornelius was ready to hear the message of the gospel.

5. Cornelius informed Peter: *"Four days ago I was fasting until this hour; and at the ninth hour I prayed in my house, and behold, a man stood before me in bright clothing."* Can we assume it was now the fifth day since Cornelius had fasted and prayed – a reminder of the fifth day and the Feast of Trumpets?

6. As Peter spoke, *'The Holy Spirit fell upon all those who heard the word.'* The granting of the Holy Spirit confirmed God was ready to bless the Gentiles, as He had blessed the sea creatures and the birds (Genesis 1:22).

Scientists now know that fish (like birds) are able to communicate with each other and they refer to this as *'Referential Signaling'*. It is a term which is not unlike communicating the gospel to others. The Holy Spirit knew Cornelius was ready to receive the gospel, which is why He told Cornelius to send for Peter. When Jew and Gentile met, Peter and Cornelius, it was to break down the wall of separation between them, apparent since the time of Moses (See Ephesians 2:11–22).

Today, the command of Jesus has been largely fulfilled. The gospel has been preached to the ends of the earth and Jerusalem, God's city that was subjugated by the nations and neglected for nearly two thousand years, has been returned to the loving care of the Jewish people (Luke 21:24). (My book, *'ISRAEL RESTORED'*, has recently been published. Please contact the Publisher for details. See page 234 for a summary).

God's instructions to the fish and the birds to multiply, and the instruction of Jesus to His disciples to make more disciples, suggests that in each case the imperative is on multiplying what God (then repeated by Jesus) commanded; for the typology can be seen with precision in the fifth Hebrew festival, the Feast of Trumpets.

The Sixth Day and the Day of Atonement

The final day of creation, the sixth day (the seventh day was set-aside as a time for God and creation to rest), is the time to consider: Does the sixth day correspond in any way to the Day of Atonement, the sixth appointed time, and if it does, what is the evidence in Genesis 1:24–31 to give credence to such a proposal?

'Then God said, "Let the earth bring forth the living creature according to its kind; cattle and creeping thing and beast of the earth, each according to its kind"; and it was so. And God made the beast of the earth according to its kind, cattle according to its kind, and everything that creeps on the earth according to its kind. And God saw that it was good. Then God said, "Let Us make man in Our image, according to Our likeness; let them have dominion over the fish of the sea, over the birds of the air, and over the cattle, over all the earth and over every creeping thing that creeps on the earth." So God created man in His own image; in the image of God He created Him; male and female He created them' (Genesis 1:24–27).

Then God saw everything that He had made, and indeed it was very good. So the evening and the morning were the sixth day (Genesis 1:31).

On the sixth day, God created man. God said: *"Let Us make man in Our image, according to Our likeness"* (Genesis 1:26). In this brief statement, there are three referrals to the plurality of God in the making of man. There are, of course, a number of Scriptures where God is described as being other than single. For example: *"You are My Son, today I have become Your Father"* (Psalm 2:7). And also in Ezekiel: *'Thus says the LORD GOD: "O house of Israel, let Us have no more of your abominations"'* (Ezekiel 44:6). His admonishment points to a plurality of Himself – yet God is one God.

That the Bible describes man as having been made on the sixth day, and the Day of Atonement is the sixth appointed time – when the high priest entered the holy-of-holies to meet with God – suggests that if God wanted to set-aside a day for His Son's birth, then these two events must be related. What took place on the sixth day, and what took place on the Day of Atonement, indicates the decision to send Jesus may well have been taken long before Genesis was written.

When God chose the way to restore His relationship with man, but without man's sin, for God is holy, God knew the initiative would have to be His. Because of man's sin in Eden (and his lack of respect for God and for obeying God's commandments), renewed fellowship with God would again only be possible if God was willing and able to bring about a work of atonement.

In the New Testament, Jesus is frequently referred to as the *'Son of God'*, but He is also referred to as the *'Son of Man'*, descriptions which are typical Hebraisms – meaning: *'Partaking of the nature of'*.

Paul's letter to the believers in Philippi refers to Jesus as being God's son, but also as a man. *'Christ Jesus, who being in the form of God, did not consider it robbery to be equal with God, but made Himself of no reputation, taking the form of a bondservant, and coming in the likeness of men* [at His birth]. *And being found in appearance as a man* [first by the shepherds], *He humbled Himself and became obedient to the point of death, even the death of the cross'* (Philippians 2:5–8).

Does this mean that when Jesus was born, He became less than God? No, of course not, *'For in Him dwells all the fullness of the Godhead bodily'* (Colossians 2:9). To see the three-fold link with the sixth day of creation, the sixth day of remembrance (the Day of Atonement), and the birth of the Lord Jesus, is to see that the birth of Jesus was intended long before Jesus was born.

God once said to Isaiah: *"For My thoughts are not your thoughts, nor are your ways My ways," says the LORD. "For as the heavens are higher than the earth, so are My ways higher than your ways, and My thoughts than your thoughts"* (Isaiah 55:8–9). God is omniscient (not prone to being reactionary) and always strategic; as seen in all of creation and in the sending of His Son.

The Seventh Day and the Feast of Tabernacles

And so we come to the final day in God's amazing plan. What did God do – what is the seventh day for?

'Thus the heavens and the earth, and all the host of them, were finished. And on the seventh day God ended His work which He had done, and He rested on the seventh day from all His work which He had done. Then God blessed the seventh day and sanctified it, because in it He rested from all His work which God had created and made' (Genesis 2:1–3).

God's seven-fold plan of salvation – as portrayed in the first seven days – is the way for mankind to return to God; and then to tabernacle with Him and to experience rest as He also rested on the seventh day.

The end of the first seven days brings us to the Feast of Tabernacles, known as: *"The Feast of Ingathering at the end of the year, when you have gathered in the fruit of your labors from the field"* (Exodus 23:16). For those who have trusted in Jesus, rest is assured when they have ended the work Jesus has given them to do. This *'rest'* is described as: *'Entering His rest'* (Hebrews 4:1). But also: *'Be diligent to enter that rest'* (Hebrews 4:11).

When Jesus went up to Jerusalem to attend the Feast of Tabernacles, and to teach in the temple, it was, *'On the last day, that great day of the feast, Jesus stood and cried out, saying, "If anyone thirsts, let him come to Me and drink. He who believes in Me, as the Scripture has said, out of his heart will flow rivers of living water"'* (John 7:37–38). His timing was superb – *'The last day!'*

Regarding what is meant for us to *'Tabernacle'* with God, Jesus said to His disciples: *"Let not your heart be troubled; you believe in God, believe also in Me. In my Father's house are many mansions; if it were not so, I would have told you. I go to prepare a place for you. And if I go and prepare a place for you, I will come again and receive you to Myself; that where I am, there you may be also"* (John 14:1–3).

The temporary shelters used by Jewish people during the Feast of Tabernacles (the *'Sukkot'*), when they give thanks for their final harvest, the fruits and the berries, after which they can enjoy a time of rest, is to be superseded by the place Jesus is preparing for those who have loved and served Him, that they may tabernacle with Him and experience the rest He has promised them.

God's Great Plan of Salvation

Thus we find in Genesis 1:1–2:3, a seven-fold blueprint of God's plan of salvation; a quintessential portrayal of the earliest foundations of the Christian faith.

1. Jesus, the *'Light of the World'*, who at the time of Passover, His life was extinguished.

2. Jesus the righteous (Unleavened Bread) Son of God, who forfeited His life for the unrighteous (leavened), that He might bring us back to God.

3. Jesus rose from the dead on the third day, a first-fruit sign He was (and is) God's Son.

4. Jesus initiated the sending of the Holy Spirit (at the time of the Feast of Weeks), enabling the reaping of a harvest of souls (Jews first) for God.

5. The commencement of the Great Commission to preach the gospel (the sounding of the trumpet at the Feast of Trumpets) to the Gentile nations.

6. The gospel is sin atoned for, as seen in the Day of Atonement, revealing why God sent Jesus to be the Saviour of the World.

7. When Jesus cried: *"It is finished"* (John 19:30) – as God also *'finished'* His work after the first six days (Exodus 2:1) – for those who trust in Jesus, they will be given rest (Feast of Tabernacles) as God rested from His work on the seventh day.

Dr Allen Wiseman

Just two weeks after I saw Jesus portrayed in Genesis 1:1 to 2:3, I met in Tel Aviv, Israel, Dr. Allen Wiseman, a Canadian born Jew and holder of a doctorate in Jewish philosophy. I explained to Dr. Wiseman how I came to believe Jesus was born on the Day of Atonement. I was surprised when Dr. Wiseman told me he had recently written a pamphlet about the link between the seven days of creation, and the seven feasts of the Lord! With his kind permission, I quote what Dr. A. Wiseman has written. (Please note his initial and his name).

'Seven holy appointed times or feasts mark the yearly, Biblical calendar. God initiated the series in Exodus 12, to be fully listed in Leviticus 23. These times represent a pattern of Scripture that begins with the seven days or periods of creation week, that are echoed by the regular weekly cycle, and further elaborated in Israel's deliverance from Egyptian slavery. As creation continues until the end of time, so to do the effects of

these seven feasts. Both the repetition of the weekly cycle and the seven yearly holidays, remind us of real past events that also point to the prophetic future. As such, these feasts are more than ordinary holidays. While the regular weekly and yearly cycles ingrain in us a down-to-earth rhythm in life, the linear process gives us an overall perspective that spans from the very beginning of creation to the ultimate completion of God's redemptive purposes.'

'Historically, because the Christian world veered away from its Jewish roots in the early centuries, the larger scope and significance of the Lord's seven feasts were often overlooked, or not sufficiently understood.'

Creation as Explained by John Metcalfe

A few weeks later I obtained Rev. John Metcalfe's book *'Creation'* (1996). Ordained under the tutelage of Dr. Martyn Lloyd-Jones, Metcalfe has seen true revival as a result of his ministry. In addition, Metcalfe has written profusely about many aspects of the Christian faith, including an explanation of the first account of creation.

Metcalf writes: *'The first account, Genesis 1:1 to 2:3, reveals the vision of creation. So that the record answers to creation as God envisioned it in terms of His eternal purpose. Although the dawning promise of the coming of Christ mysteriously appeared in the first account of creation in Genesis, in fact Christ Himself in person, made manifest in the flesh, was not to appear until aeons later. The very wording of the first account of what happened at creation is framed so as to intimate the vision in the mind of God of and for His Son in the New Testament.'*

Rev. Metcalfe concludes: *'For the truth is that hidden in the records of the creation, lies the revelation of Jesus Christ, quite apart from the record of Adam.'*

Jesus Concealed – Jesus Revealed

God has never been disorganized, for He has a plan, and its details can be found in the Hebrew Foundations of the Christian Faith as Jesus explained: *'In the Law of Moses and the Prophets and the Psalms'* (Luke 24:44). God's plan is one that involves Himself, His Son and the Holy Spirit. The first blue-print of this plan is to be found not in the New Testament, but in the first two chapters of the Old Testament, for it is here we see Jesus concealed. Eventually, Jesus would solve man's problem – his sin and his separation from God – and so the solution to the problem is what we find in the New Testament, for here we see Jesus revealed.

Thanks and Praise

In ancient Hebrew, the word *'Thanks'* is the same as the word for *'Praise'*. Therefore, and in the words of the apostle Paul, as we consider who Jesus is, may we join with Paul and say: *"Thanks* [Praise] *be to God for His indescribable gift"* (2 Corinthians 9:15).

On the next four pages there are fifteen questions which are based on this study. Suggested answers can be found on pages 226–227.

Study 9 Questions – Creation Week

1. On the first day God said: *"Let there be light."* Regarding Himself, what did Jesus say about light? (John 8:12).

ANSWER: _____

2. What happened to this light when Jesus died at Passover; the first of the seven festivals?

ANSWER: _____

3. On the second day God divided the waters from below from the waters above. The second Hebrew festival is known as the festival of Unleavened Bread. Where is division seen in this ancient Hebrew festival? (Exodus 12:20).

ANSWER: _____

_____

4. How does the apostle Paul describe leaven? How does he describe unleavened?

   In each case, two words. (1 Corinthians 5:6–8).

ANSWER: (1) _____

(2) _____

5. On the third day God caused the grasses, herbs and trees to bear seed and fruit. What is the third Hebrew festival called? On which day of the week is it celebrated? (Leviticus 23:11).

ANSWER: _____

6. In Hebrew the number three is a linked to resurrection. After spending three days and three nights in the tomb, on which day of the week did Jesus rise from the dead? (John 20:1).

ANSWER: _____

7. The Feast of Firstfruits, the third feast, is held on the first day of the week, and Jesus rose from the dead on the first day of the week. Therefore, by the timing of His resurrection, how do you see Jesus as being *'The Light of the world'*?

ANSWER: _____

8. On the fourth day God created the sun and the moon to be for *'Seasons, Days and Years'*. In Genesis 1:14, what other factor are we told the sun and the moon were to be used for?

ANSWER: _____

9. The fourth Hebrew festival is called the Feast of Weeks. Why is it important we recall the sun and moon were created on the fourth day?

ANSWER: _____

_____

10. Many years later, in the city of Jerusalem, what took place on the occasion of this fourth Hebrew festival which paved the way for the gospel to be preached to the world? (Acts 2).

ANSWER: _____

11. On the fifth day God's first command was for the sea creatures and the birds to fill the seas and the earth. Soon after the day of Pentecost, the gospel was preached for the first time to the Gentiles. This corresponded to Jesus' final command. Describe this command? (Acts 1:8).

ANSWER: _____

12. On the sixth day God said: *"Let Us make man in Our image."* The sixth time of remembrance is known as the Day of Atonement. Do you think it appropriate/not appropriate that the Day of Atonement should be remembered as being a suitable day for the birth of Jesus?

ANSWER: _____

13. On the seventh day God rested from His work. What is the seventh Hebrew festival called? (Leviticus 23:34).

ANSWER: _____

14. In Hebrews 4:9–10, it describes us as entering God's rest. What should our attitude to this be? (Hebrews 4:11).

ANSWER: _____

15. On the occasion when Jesus visited Jerusalem to celebrate the Feast of Tabernacles, He cried out saying: *"If anyone thirsts, let him come to Me and drink. He who believes in Me…"* Complete His statement (John 7:37–38).

ANSWER: _____

_____

_____

****

WHAT'S IN A NAME?

I include this section (although it was not part of my lectures for the students in Moldova), as it is relevant to these studies. It concerns a man who although he may be a little obscure, he was filled with the Holy Spirit.

When God gave Moses instructions about how Israel's tabernacle was to be constructed, He also identified the person He had previously chosen to carry out the work. *'Then the LORD spoke to Moses, saying: "See, I have called by name Bezalel the son of Uri, the son of Hur, of the tribe of Judah. And I have filled him with the Spirit of God in wisdom, in understanding, in knowledge, and in all manner of workmanship"'* (Exodus 31:1–3). Although others would have assisted him in his work, it appears Bezalel, using his carpentry and metal working skills, completed one important task himself. *'Then Bezalel made the ark of acacia wood'* (Exodus 37:1). When it was completed, the ark of acacia wood was placed in the tabernacle's holy-of-holies for use (only) on the Day of Atonement.

The Day of Atonement's focus on Bezalel's work in the making of the Ark of the Covenant looked to the future, to Jesus' birth, and His need for a suitable resting place. However, during the Second Temple era, there was no longer an Ark of the Covenant in the temple's holy-of-holies, and so an alternative was needed.

The manger, in which Mary placed her new-born Son (as angels looked down and worshipped – likewise, the cherubim on the Ark of the Covenant looked down), was a humble alternative to the Ark of the Covenant. Also, compare Joseph who was betrothed to Mary, to Bezalel. In Hebrew, Bezalel's name means: *'IN THE SHADOW OF GOD'* (An important point, and one not to be missed).

1. God commissioned both Bezalel and Joseph to become involved in His plan(s) of salvation.

2. Bezalel and Joseph were both carpenters.

3. Bezalel and Joseph were both from the tribe of Judah (Exodus 31:2 & Luke 2:4).

4. At His birth, the rightful place for Jesus to have been born was in the temple's of holy-of-holies, and on the Day of Atonement where Bezalel's work had once been located. However, God selected a more modest place for Jesus' birth, He who was destined to become our High Priest.

5. And Joseph, having been chosen by God to act as the foster father to Jesus, acted like Bezalel – *'IN THE SHADOW OF GOD'*.

At the time when Moses first set up the tabernacle, *'He took the testimony* [the two tablets of stone on which God had written the words of the Ten Commandments,

Exodus 34:28] *and put it into the ark'* (Exodus 40:20). *'Then the cloud covered the tabernacle of meeting, and the glory of the LORD filled the tabernacle. And Moses was not able to enter the tabernacle of meeting, because the cloud rested above it, and the glory of the LORD filled the tabernacle'* (Exodus 40:34–35).

The cloud which stood above the tabernacle and the Ark of the Covenant (which had been made by Bezalel), in which Moses placed the testimony, the word of God written by the hand of God – as Jesus is also *'The Word of God'* (Revelation 19:13) – was but a prelude of what would take place later, when a star guided the wise men to Bethlehem, *'till it came and stood over where the young child was'* (Matthew 2:9). By the sign of a star, wise men visited Jesus, the brightness of God's glory, who was destined to become *'A Holy Testimony'*, the infant child who Mary laid in a manger.

In his introduction to the fourth Gospel, John wrote: *'In the beginning was the Word, and the Word was with God and the Word was God. He* [the Lord Jesus] *was in the beginning with God'* (John 1:1). Jesus was, is, and always will be *'A Holy Testimony'* (Hebrew 13:8 – *'Jesus Christ is the same yesterday, today and forever'*), and Mary placed Him in a manger. Following the birth of Jesus, without any doubt, the Ark of the Covenant would have been a much more suitable resting place for Jesus, for it both symbolized and pre-figured the way for the introduction of the New Covenant.

Might Bezalel be an additional *sign* for the timing of the birth of Jesus? I believe so, because Bezalel is the first person we read of who was filled with the Holy Spirit (Exodus 31:3). The reason he was, was because Bezalel was chosen to oversee the building of the tabernacle. Bezalel also made the Ark of the Covenant and the linen vestments the priests wore (a senior version of the swaddling cloths Mary used for wrapping Jesus in) both of which were featured on the Day of Atonement when divine service was carried out by one individual, Israel's high priest. This is the one who the writer of the book of Hebrews describes, Jesus came to replace.

'Therefore, holy brethren, partakers of the heavenly calling, consider the apostle and high priest of our confession, Christ Jesus, who was faithful to Him who appointed Him, as Moses also was faithful in all his house. For this One has been counted worthy of more glory than Moses, inasmuch as He who built the house has more glory than the house. For every house is built by someone, but He who built all things is God' (Hebrews 3:1–4).

The Chief Cornerstone – A Firm Foundation

Thus: *'The stone which the builders rejected* [Jesus] *has become the chief corner stone.'* Concerning this bedrock of the Christian faith, the Psalmist went on to say: *'This was the Lord's doing; it is marvelous in our eyes'* (Psalm 118:22–23). Amen, and amen.

ANSWERS

Study 1 – The Exodus from the Garden of Eden and from Egypt

1. The freeing of the Hebrew people from their four hundred years of slavery in Egypt.

2. Unleavened bread represents righteousness. Leavened bread represents unrighteousness.

3. Jesus was without no sin; no unrighteousness.

4. Adam. The Garden of Eden. The Tree of Life. The Tree of the Knowledge of Good and Evil. The Serpent. The Temptation of Man. The Fall of Man. (The above lists seven things which are not named in the first account of creation).

5. God killed an animal in order to use its skin to clothe Adam and his wife Eve.

6. Atonement.

7. To do the things Jesus has asked us to do and to keep God's commandments.

8. Egypt, and for four hundred years.

9. Pharaoh saw them as a possible threat to his country and wanted to limit their numbers.

10. On the fourteenth day of the first month.

11. (I am the Lord your God, who) *"...brought you out of the land of Egypt, out of the house of bondage."*

12. On the tenth day. It was the day they were told to select a lamb for Passover.

13. To sanctify themselves – to set themselves apart. On the ninth day of the first month.

14. Mary anointed the feet of Jesus with costly oil of spikenard. She then wiped His feet with her hair. Jesus said she did this as an act of sanctification for His death, five days later. i.e., on the 14th day of the first month.

15. A Sample answer: When I repented of my sin and asked Jesus to forgive me, Jesus came into my life. I know Jesus has set me free from my sin, so that I might follow and serve Him for the rest of my life.

****

ANSWERS

Study 2 – Joseph and Jesus

1. Matthew 1:18–25.

2. Joseph – by his brothers.
   Jesus – by Caiaphas, the high priest (also a fellow Jew).

3. The Roman soldiers who had crucified Jesus.
   In Psalm 22:18.

4. Judas Iscariot sold Jesus for thirty pieces of silver.
   Matthew 26:14–15.

5. Reuben: In the pit where Joseph's brothers had placed him.
   The women: In the tomb where Jesus was laid.

6. Jacob: *"A wild beast has devoured him."*
   Jesus: Dogs, a lion, and wild oxen.

7. Joseph: *The LORD was with Joseph.*
   Jesus: *'God was in Christ…'*

8. Joseph: Joseph was tempted to commit adultery.
   Jesus: Like Joseph, Satan tempted Jesus to break God's Law; His Commandments.

9. Bread and Wine.

10. Pharaoh said: *"Can we find such a one as this, a man in whom is the Spirit of God?"*

11. He quoted Isaiah 61:1–2. Because as Jesus said: *"The Spirit of the LORD is upon Me..."*

12. Joseph: The people cried out: *"Bow the knee!"*
    Jesus: The people cried out: *"Blessed is He who comes in the name of the LORD! The King of Israel!"*

13. Joseph was thirty.
    Jesus was thirty.

14. *"He must increase, but I must decrease."*

15. Eleven disciples – the same number as Joseph's brothers.

****

ANSWERS

Study 3 – The Ark of the Covenant

1. Yes – for they must have been preserved for a reason, or reasons.

2. In the Tabernacle's holy-of-holies.

3. God's provision for His people during their forty years of wandering in the wilderness.

4. God elected and gave authority to Aaron to act as His chosen representative.

5. The way for us to respect God, to obey His commandments, and to live in harmony with others.

6. The Ten Commandments.

7. Through Jesus, because He gave Himself to be our atonement sacrifice. Jesus is the *'New and Living Way'* for us to approach God.

8. Aaron's Rod.

9. Three times.

10. The golden jar of Manna.

11. For the bread of God… *"…is He who comes down from heaven and gives life to the world. I am the bread of life. He who comes to Me shall never hunger, and he who believes in Me shall never thirst."*

12. Joseph said: *"So it was not you* [Joseph's brothers] *who sent me here, but God."*

13. Joseph said: *"God has made me a father to Pharaoh, and a ruler throughout the land of Egypt."*

14. That he might provide food (grain) for his father Jacob, his brothers and their families.

15. Its depth. What was on the inside of the Ark of the Covenant was important; because the three items represented three aspects of the Lord Jesus.

****

ANSWERS

Study 4 – The Tabernacle

1. For God to dwell in the midst of His people and for the people to draw near to God.

2. The righteousness (or Holiness) of God in the midst of His people.

3. The life of the flesh is in the blood. Without the shedding of blood there can be no forgiveness.

4. Jesus took a basin and in it He poured water. He then washed His disciples' feet.

5. The holy place and the holy-of-holies.

6. Seven.

7. The table of showbread and the incense altar.

8. The veil.

9. The veil was torn in two – from top to bottom. This indicates the way into God's presence is now open, because Jesus has enabled a new way for Jews and Gentiles to draw near to God.

10. The Glory of the Lord illuminated the holy-of-holies.

11. The Ark of the Covenant.

12. On the Day of Atonement.

13. Jesus is in the Most Holy Place – Heaven –
    having shed His own blood for our sin.

14. To rebuild the temple might lead to a return to
    former religious practices, such as animal
    sacrifices, which would be an affront to God; for
    Jesus gave His life for our sin.

15. In the inner sanctuary of the temple; the Most
    Holy Place.
    God said: *"My name shall be there."*

****

ANSWERS

Study 5 – When was Jesus Born?

1. Jesus is God's Son and He existed before His physical birth which took place in Bethlehem.

2. Micah.

3. Seven times.

4. In Daniel 9:27, it says: *'Half a Week'* – which is half of seven years, or three- and-a-half years.

5. On the eve of Passover – about three o'clock in the afternoon of the 14th day of the first month.

6. God.

7. 1, Passover. 2, The Feast of Unleavened Bread. 3, The Feast of Firstfruits. 4, The Feast of Weeks. 5, The Feast of Trumpets. 6, The Day of Atonement. 7, The Feast of Tabernacles.

****

ANSWERS

Study 6 – Psalm 23

1. A lamb.

2. The festival of Unleavened Bread.

3. The Garden of Gethsemane in the Kidron Valley, and/or Calvary. (Ideally, both).

4. Jesus broke bread at a table and on the occasion of the Hebrew festival of Firstfruits.

5. The Feast of Weeks.

6. It is God's love and His kindness – *'GOOD NEWS'* as seen in the Hebrew Feast of Trumpets.

7. The Day of Atonement. First an animal, later it was Jesus, for it describes the life span – from birth to death – of the sacrifice which was offered for the sins of those who wish to know God.

8. *"And I will dwell in the house of the LORD – Forever."*

****

ANSWERS

Study 7 – Hanukkah

1. (1) In the beginning. (2) There was darkness.
    (3) There was light.

2. John the Baptist.

3. The Feast of Dedication.

4. 40 weeks.

5. 40 weeks.

6. *'As for God, His way is perfect; the word of the
    LORD is proven…'*

****

ANSWERS

Study 8 – Our High Priest

1. He is making intercession (praying) for us.

2. To serve God and to serve others, and to keep themselves holy.

3. He purged – or cleansed – us of our sin.

4. Into Heaven's Most Holy Place – the original of the Tabernacle's holy-of-holies.

5. The Day of Atonement.

6. *"You are My Son, today I became Your Father."*

7. (1) Yes. (2) Yes.

****

ANSWERS

Study 9 – Creation Week

1. *"I am the light of the world."*

2. The Light of the world was extinguished.

3. *"You shall eat nothing leavened; in all your dwellings you shall eat unleavened bread."*

4. Leaven: Malice and Wickedness.
   Unleavened: Sincerity and truth.

5. The Feast of Firstfruits.
   On the first day of the week.

6. On the first day of the week.

7. Jesus fulfills God's declaration on the first day of the week and by His resurrection continues to be *'The Light of the world'*.

8. Signs.

9. It is because the Sun and the Moon control the Earth's days, weeks, years and seasons.

10. The disciples were filled with the Holy Spirit.

11. The disciples were to go and preach the gospel to the whole world.

12. Appropriate.

13. The Feast of Tabernacles.

14. To be diligent to enter God's rest.

15. *"As the Scripture has said, out of his heart will flow rivers of living water."*

****

ABOUT THE AUTHOR

I was born in December 1943, but it was not until 1953 that my parents, my brother, my sister and I, started to attend Cranleigh Baptist Church (Surrey), and it was here that we accepted Jesus as our Saviour.

My sister Clemaine had a very close relationship with Jesus, but as a result of a drowning accident, Clemaine died at an early age on our family farm. At the time of her death, Clemaine had only recently started work in Guildford, Surrey, having just celebrated her fifteenth birthday. Although Clemaine's death led to much family sorrow, our faith in God was never questioned.

Two years later, I decided what to do when I left school. Six months later (June 1959) – I was just fifteen-and-a-half – I joined the Royal Air Force to train as an aircraft electrician.

Initially, as I moved from adolescence to adulthood, my faith was my bedrock. Arrival in adulthood, however, can coincide with distractions, and it was weakness on my part that allowed other things to divert me away from Jesus. Thankfully, the distractions failed to rob me of my faith and the Holy Spirit needed only seven words (spoken by John the Baptist) to bring me back to Jesus. *"He must increase, but I must decrease."*

Fourteen years in the Royal Air Force was followed by ten years with Rank Xerox as a photo-copier service engineer. Photo-copiers then gave way to *'Open Doors with Brother Andrew'*, a Christian organisation based in Holland that was involved in taking Bibles to Christians in countries where Christianity was restricted; such as China and the countries of Eastern Europe. At the end of my time with Open Doors (seven years), I joined Sun Life of Canada to train as a financial consultant (ten years). In the year 2000, I qualified as an Independent Financial Adviser.

With retirement looming I decided to try a new venture, and so I started *'Plus One Garden Services'* to help local people with their gardens and properties. I called this venture *'Plus One'*, because of who Jesus is.

Many years ago, not long after I re-dedicated my life to Jesus, I remember attending an evening service at my home church in Cranleigh. The speaker took for his text Hebrews 4:16 – *'Let us therefore come boldly to the throne of grace, that we may obtain mercy and find grace to help in time of need.* It is a Scripture I have not forgotten, and whenever I read it, it takes me back to Cranleigh.

Since that evening, and whenever I read Hebrews, I am struck by its many references to the Old Testament, and because of this, my interest in both the Old Testament and Israel has been stimulated.

In one sense, I see Hebrews as the book on which the two historical periods of our Bibles are joined – B.C.E & C.E. Also, the Jewish people span and connect these two periods. This may explain my fascination with the foundations of the Christian faith.

From when Janet and I were married (1966), we have been interested in the world-wide history of the Jewish people and the nation of Israel. The Bible has been our primary means of understanding Israel, for it is here we have learnt about God's covenant with Abraham and his descendants.

Janet and I have visited Israel a number of times and have always enjoyed our visits. We have discovered that Israel is a country you can easily fall in love with, and its people, mostly Jews and Arabs, are friendly and welcoming. In June 2007, we visited Israel with friends, and it was here that I had a very remarkable experience in Jerusalem.

As we were passing through the Arab quarter of the Old City, I dallied to take photographs. While scanning the buildings of this ancient city, where Jesus once walked, I noticed an elderly Arab man. Unavoidably, like the beam of a laser, our eyes met, yet I had no knowledge of his intention; if indeed he had one.

With a sense of purpose, the man walked towards me; then, as we faced each other only inches apart, the stranger took hold of my right arm and looked into my eyes. His look was friendly, and so I was not afraid. Next, his lips moved, as he spoke four words: *"You are a Jew!"* I was dumbfounded, rooted to the spot! The friendly man then removed his hand from my arm and walked away – never to be seen again. His timing was forty years to the day from when Jerusalem's Old City was returned to the custodianship of the Jewish people.

Did his announcement change my life? I'm not sure, but I've not forgotten him! For many years, I have believed that in my family's history, Jewish antecedents do exist, but I've not pursued the matter. In believing that an attitude of pragmatism is in-tune with my thought life, I feel my usefulness to God is to seek to do His will – and to try to understand the foundations of my faith as portrayed in the Hebrew Scriptures. This is why the foundations of what Christians believe is important – together with the history of the Jewish people – and why I feel my calling is to write about these things.

What I have tried to convey in these studies (my reason also for visiting Moldova to share these studies with the students at the University) will, I trust, assist you in your faith; and therefore why the Hebrew Foundations of the Christian Faith are so essentially important.

David Hamshire
January 2017

BIBLIOGRAPHY

Booker, R. *'Celebrating Jesus in the Biblical Feasts'* (Shippensburg, PA: Destiny Image, 2009) page 181.

Bullinger, E. W. *'Number in Scripture'* (Grand Rapids, MI: Kregel, 1967) pages 23, 135–136, 243.

Davis. D. *'The Elijah Legacy'.* (The life and times of Elijah. The prophetic significance for Israel, Islam and the Church in the last days). Kehilat HaCarmel, P.O. Box 7004, Haifa 31070, Israel.

Foster. C. *'TRACKING THE ARK OF THE COVENANT'.* (Monarch Books, a publishing imprint of Lion Hudson plc. 2007). Pages 207–208.

Heschel, A. J. *'The Sabbath'* (New York, NY: Farrar, Straus and Giroux, 1951).

Holland, T. *'Hope for the Nations — Paul's letter to the Romans. A Corporate Reading'* (London: Apostolos, 2015). Page 169.

Israel, A. and R. Chaim, eds. *'Carta's Illustrated Encyclopedia of the Holy Temple in Jerusalem'* (Jerusalem: The Temple Institute Carta, 2005). Page 61.

Keegstra, J. *'God's Prophetic Feasts'* (International Christian Embassy Jerusalem – ICEJ – 2007). Page 49.

Leupold, H. C. *'Exposition of the Psalms'* (London: Evangelical Press, 1969). Pages 208–215.

Metcalfe, J. *'Creation'* (Penn: John Metcalfe, 1996). Pages 29–63.

Pink, A. W. P. *'Gleanings in Genesis'* (Seaside, OR: Watchmaker, 1951). Pages 20–26.

Stern, D. H. *'The Complete Jewish Bible'* (Clarksville, MD: Jewish New Testament Publications 1998).

Wiseman, A. *'The Feasts — Seven, Holy, Appointed Times of The Lord'* in an email from Dr Wiseman, quoted with permission.

Wright. T. *'HEBREWS for EVERYONE'* (Society for Promoting Christian Knowledge – SPCK – 2003). Page 93.

****

ISRAEL RESTORED

My other book which is being published by Apostolos Publishing, concerns the return to the Land of Israel of the Jewish people. Its title is: *'ISRAEL RESTORED'*.

When others show appreciation for the work we do, it's encouraging, and I include below part of the Foreword for this book. Please contact the Publisher for details.

ISRAEL RESTORED – an extract from the Foreword

The name *'Israel'* usually provokes a reaction of some sort. In today's world, the reaction is often negative, with many people regarding the nation of Israel as an obstacle to world peace and peace in the Middle East.

Among the Christian community, there is often a similar polarising in people's opinions of Jews as a people and as a nation. On one hand there are a few who are deeply envious of the Jews and their traditions, and would give anything to be able to become Jewish by birth, and at the other extreme are those who espouse *'Replacement Theology'* and regard Israel as a distraction compared with the true church and God's purposes for it. The views held are often entrenched and unshakable. Israel provokes a deeply held passion in people's hearts!

This book has been written by someone who is also a man of strong passions – especially when it comes to the Jews and their nation, Israel. David Hamshire has a passion which drives him to discover a true and an eternal viewpoint with which to regard Israel. In looking for arguments to establish his belief in the central place that Israel plays in the purposes of God, David examines Scripture with the keen eye of a detective, and having found gold nuggets of truth, he then seeks to substantiate them by looking at the history of Israel the nation and the Jews as a people and noting how history has fully endorsed the validity of prophetic words found in Scripture.

The result is a thesis which presents watertight arguments, insightful interpretations, and consistent evidence of a nation which still occupies a place in the heart and the purposes of God.

'ISRAEL RESTORED' is an argument for the place of Israel in the heart of God, which is detailed, and persuasive. David presents a coordinated stream of scriptural support for the survival of Israel against all odds, and the place of Israel in these end times. After reading this book, it would be difficult to hold an anti-Semitic view of Israel, or to still consider that the emergence of the church has done away with Israel as far as God is concerned. I commend this book to you.

Richard G. Sexton